CONCERN FOR THE CHURCH

CONCERN
FOR THE CHURCH

THEOLOGICAL INVESTIGATIONS XX

by

KARL RAHNER

Translated by

EDWARD QUINN

CROSSROAD · NEW YORK

1981
The Crossroad Publishing Company
575 Lexington Avenue, New York, NY 10022

A translation of selected articles from
SCHRIFTEN ZUR THEOLOGIE, XIV
published by Verlagsanstalt Benziger & Co. A.G., Einsiedeln

This translation
© Darton, Longman & Todd Ltd, 1981
First published 1981

Library of Congress Catalog Card Number: 61–8189
ISBN: 0–8245–0027–X
Printed in the U.S.A.

CONTENTS

PART ONE

Faith and Church

1

COURAGE FOR AN ECCLESIAL CHRISTIANITY

T HE QUESTION as to why I am a Christian is radically different from, say, that of a preference to live in one country rather than in another. The second question refers to a particular aspect of life which must be linked with other, quite different aspects: it must find its place within a co-ordinated system. But a really living Christianity involves the totality of human existence. A Christian life therefore cannot be justified by establishing its place within a greater and more comprehensive co-ordinated system, the latter being already accepted as legitimate. How then is it possible to answer this question at all? This is particularly difficult today when—as distinct from former times—scarcely anything is generally accepted that can also be assumed to be approved by the person who raises the question in a critical spirit. Anyone who tries to extort an answer to a question like this, about a totality of existence and reality must—to be fair—really allow for the fact that the answer will be very fragmentary and perhaps fail to deal with the very point about which the questioner, rightly from his own standpoint, is inquiring.

For me the self and the world create a question to which there can never be a complete answer. It is obvious to me that even in the most distant future of the history of human experience and—secondarily—of science there will never be a point at which all questions will be answered, all problems cleared up and finally settled. I am really surprised how and on what grounds probably most of my contemporaries share this conviction of mine, even those who deny that what or whom I call God exists. These people really ought to think it possible in principle to get behind each and every thing, behind the particular reality that I am

3

myself; that ultimately everything—since it is merely the sum-total of such particularities—can be seen through and then allowed to drop back into its banality, in the last resort into nothingness. That very nothingness, to which questions of this kind would bring us, need not raise any problems nor does it require any explanation, if it really is nothingness and if the term 'nothingness' is not at all mysterious and as such does not mean something entirely different.

But what encompasses and permeates me is the eternal mystery, the infinite mystery, which is anything but the sum-total of the scraps left over of what is not currently known or has not yet been experienced: the mystery which in its infinity and density is both farthest from and most deeply rooted in the thousand fragmented realities which we describe as our world of experience. This mystery is present and finds expression by remaining silent; it is unperturbed when people claim that talking about it is nothing but idle chatter. I can understand the indignation and irritability of those who make this claim. As soon as a person fails to come with loving adoration to this mystery, which silently encompasses everything, it becomes an irritant. It is present and cannot be brought into a system. It seems only to be silent and to dissolve all our own clarities and certainties. If we do not lovingly yield to it, we can only spend our time in indignantly denying it; or we suppress it, taking refuge in everyday affairs and attaching to these more importance than their fleeting and fading existence can yield.

This mystery, which provides the ground of all individual reality and scope and background for all knowledge and freedom, I call God. It does not have to be proved circumstantially, even though those who try to prove it may well reflect on the fact that we always tacitly assume it and give it a name whenever we begin to speak about a thousand and one things in ordinary conversation or in the lecture halls of universities. If I pause and remain silent, allowing all the many individual realities of my life to subside into their one ground and all individual questions to be reduced to *that* question which cannot be answered through all the individual questions taken together but itself permits the infinite mystery to stand out, then the mystery is present and I am in the last resort no longer disturbed by whatever sceptical opinions a rationalistic science may choose to express on the subject. I do not think then that I am lost in irrational 'feelings', but that I have reached the point of the mind, of reason and understanding, at which all rationality arises in the very first place.

I do not despise the traditional proofs of God; I read them as meaning-ful and necessary, but also secondary interpretations and verbalizations of that experience in which I come silently before the infinite mystery. The tremendous, earth-shattering experience is that I can approach this all-encompassing, all-sustaining and permeating mystery, setting all things at a distance and yet regaining all things; I can address it, I can pray. I know that the occurrence of such a prayerful approach is itself the act of this mystery; but by this very fact I am in the presence of this mystery, distinct from it, placed there in my own reality, so that, if I approach it, I do not cease to be but I come to share precisely in this infinite mystery. In what Christians know as grace, I learn that this mystery, in order to be itself, does not need merely to place me at an infinite distance, but gives itself as our fulfilment.

The Christian is forbidden (a unique prohibition, which must be taken quite seriously) to be content with less than the infinite fullness of God; forbidden to make himself at home definitively in the finite or to become absorbed in its limitations, to assume with false modesty that God cannot really take seriously the finite creature in all its relativity. The world did not only begin to become aware of itself in man (and elsewhere, for all I know), but God himself began to come to man and man to come to God. There may in future be still thousands of evolutionary peaks, qualita-tive leaps and so on, which do not yet exist but are still to come. But the infinite, unsurpassable self-promise of God to man is here, penetrates everything, is the innermost entelechy and dynamic force of the world. In this business of course God does not cease to be the ultimate dynamic force and entelechy of the world and its history; we might say that the 'Big Bang' proclaimed, not the birth of God himself, but our own begin-ning. Otherwise God would simply not be himself.

It is part of the mystery that we can 'need' it only when it does not 'need' us. Only in the act of love on both sides can we say that God could not live without us. For it is only in this act that we receive in such a way that what is received is absolutely released. This is the mystery of love and this love is the mystery that has promised itself to us. When this self-promise of God makes its impact on the personal spirit of man, directs the latter's dynamic force on God's immediacy itself and makes God in himself (even though *as* the incomprehensible mystery) the goal and also the dynamic force of the human mind and its history, then what we properly call Christian revelation is already present, albeit still in an implicit and non-verbalized sense. This (as a disclosure of an infinite horizon, as a movement toward the infinite mystery as such, as a freedom transcending all particularities) has existed as a secret force in the whole history of human freedom wherever man has accepted in thousands of forms the incomprehensible mystery of God. It has been particularly effective in the whole length and breadth of the history of religion. Although in this history which makes objective, verbalizes and institutionalizes God's revelation in the sense just indicated, although in this objectification what is really meant fails to find adequate expression or is debased, the Christian has nevertheless the right and duty to look reverently toward the history of religion in its breadth and length, since the Spirit of God in the divine self-communication is always active there and continually fills man with an ultimate reverence and an unconditional devotion to the infinite mystery of his life. Because I consider the history of religion under this aspect and am aware of an ultimate unity in it, despite all its diversity and disintegration into contradictions, it does not infect me with that sceptical relativism of many contemporaries who can see religion only as a concoction of primitive states of consciousness, which is slowly dying out. Many one-sided and inadequate objectifications of this fundamental immediacy of the mind to God may be allowed to die out. The threat here is only to the corruption, not to the essence of religion.

I look confidently to the future of religion. If—this of course is an absurd idea—man were to evolve, evolve backwards as it were, to become a being without any yearning for the absolute, without 'metaphysics', to become merely a clever animal or the subject of his own computer, then this would only mean that the end of humanity had come, albeit in a hitherto unexpected fashion: an end which, as such, the believer had always regarded as part of his creed to expect. This end would not amount to a negative judgement on the previous history of religion as the history of an infinite hope. It would be a deliberately planned suicide of humanity, proving those to be right who had lived and believed previously. A suicide is not a judgement pronounced by a higher authority against life. The future history of religion and thus also the history of the Church may produce hitherto completely inconceivable forms of religion; it is difficult to say what the place will look like which a verbalized and institutionalized relationship of man to the eternal mystery will occupy. But as long as man is the man of God's infinite mystery, there will also be religion, which in some way will be attested in the ordinary course of life. Whether the number of those who live their religion in a socially institutionalized form will be greater or less as compared with the total number of human beings is a question to which I have no answer, but which has no fundamental significance for the person whose conscience obliges him to accept such a social expression of his religion. That Christianity as such will survive is a question which must be discussed in what follows.

My Christianity however means not only radical frankness in adoration, devotion and love for the ineffable mystery of God; it has not only what we might call a transcendental, 'pneumatological' character. My Christianity has also and essentially an historical dimension. For it acknowledges that this self-offering of the infinite mystery as fulfilment of man is not only the God-given uttermost and most radical opportunity of man for the history of his freedom, but (at least as seen in relation to the totality of the history of mankind) is also in virtue of this offering victoriously established in the world and has already been manifested in its irreversibility and in its victory in history. This historical event, in which God's offer to mankind became irreversible and is also historically palpable in this victory, is what Christian faith finds in Jesus Christ. It was this One, crucified and risen, who also proclaimed this irreversible promise by God of himself by proclaiming the immediate advent of God's Kingdom; it was he who in his unity with God and in his unconditional solidarity with all men was also aware of himself as the event of this now irremovable closeness of God to the world, who upheld the reality of this advent even when plunged into the emptiness and impotence of death and was encountered as the one who in this death as the one and complete surrender to the mystery really came with his whole existence to be with God, vindicated, encountered as the 'Risen One'. For me Jesus is the promise—no longer to be deferred or revoked—by God of himself to me in history: the ultimate unsurpassable, irrevocable Word of God, the WORD. It is in this light that I gain access to the meaning and credibility of classical Christology, of an incarnational and descendence Christology such as can be found already in the New Testament. In this light the classical Christology of Ephesus and Chalcedon has no mythological implications, even though I must admit that the Christology of many devout fellow-Christians and sometimes that of the Church's official representatives, despite their verbal orthodoxy, do not seem to me to be entirely free from mythological overtones.

To be honest, I have the impression that a proposition like 'Jesus is God' can be ineffably true and productive of salvation but that it can also be terribly misunderstood as a result of over-simplification. In the first sense it is a proposition about a unique unity, in the second it suggests an identity and can be understood only in a heterodox fashion as a shibboleth of orthodoxy, although there are some who feel they must sacrifice reason in order to assert this identity. In Christology also (with the Council of Chalcedon) it is possible to be much more rational than many people think. The ultimate and *most authentic* mystery of Christology is implied anyway in what we expect, what we may and must expect for all of us: that God as himself can impart himself to man without having to be represented by a creaturely reality and without man himself being dissolved into nothingness in this communication. Consequently my faith in my own fulfilment in God himself and faith in God's 'becoming man' in Jesus are closely linked for me; they belong to the one fundamental persuasion that God, without ceasing to be the infinite mystery, willed to be a God of ineffable closeness and does not revoke this will. Christology and pneumatology are linked indissolubly together in Christian faith. The fact that the historical manifestation of the irrevocable union of God and the world took place precisely in Jesus Christ is something that cannot of course be deduced speculatively but is part of the indissoluble facticity and singularity of history. Nevertheless I can understand that the real encounter with the Absolute, if it is not merely conceived but accepted and realized, occurs in the facticity of history and not solely in the abstract dimension of ideas.

We can love ideas and speculation, we can regard these things as part of authentic human existence, we must not depreciate them as superfluous luxuries and pastimes. But even if such an ascent to the heights of the spirit were to lead to full 'illumination', in which all veils of illusory perishability seem to fall away, this illumination as the high point of the spirit would still have to go through the night of death in order to become definitive and credible. And into that night a person would have to take everything—even though it is changed—that he is and has, his whole history with body and soul. The way of transcendence and mysticism is at an end only when the way of history ends at death. And that is why I look to him who in history has died with and for me and in whom, with an immense number of my Christian brethren, I have the courage to trust (a trust that no one elsewhere in history dares to demand from me) that this death has passed into the life of God himself. I am never merely an idea; I cannot leave history out of my idea. Consequently I know that I cannot get away from the history of Jesus, although it is inevitably burdened with all the relativity of historical reality and all the obscurity of historical knowledge.

Since I am a human being and a Christian, in the last resort it is obvious to me that I am a Christian in the Church, an ecclesial Christian. I do not want to 'socialize' thinking and free decision, to surrender understanding and freedom in a collective. But I cannot consider myself so important that my own conviction would be as radically important to me as faith must be when it involves a total life's decision which is *a priori* meant to be mine alone. If religion involves what is most real in man and man in his wholeness, then it cannot *a priori* be merely what is individual and the innermost reality of the individual person alone. Religion must be my own proper and free conviction, must be capable of being experienced at the very heart of existence. But this existence is itself found only in a community and society, being revealed in giving and receiving. Moreover Christianity is a historical religion bound up with the one Jesus Christ. I heard of him only through the Church and not otherwise. Hence I cannot be content with a purely private Christianity which would repudiate its origins. Attachment to the Church is the price I pay for this historical origin. We have still not by any means explained all or even the most important reasons for a Christian's attachment to the Church. But these must suffice.

An ecclesial Christian of this kind must of course be aware of the historicity of the Church. He knows therefore about all the far-too-human and inhuman aspects of what has happened in the Church 'in head and members', in the past and in the present. A Christian who believes that the Church truly comes from Jesus Christ and consequently that it is the basic sacrament of salvation for the whole world, in face of this only too often very human history of the Church, cannot simply ingenuously point to other historical structures and appeal to the fact that it is a history of feeble human beings who behave atrociously everywhere on the stage of world history; what he ought to do is to hope and expect the victory of grace, which the Church even in its visible manifestation is meant to promise to the world, to be revealed in radiant splendour in its own history. Here is the revelation which only the gloomy despiser of mankind can overlook as a matter of principle. But the Christian could wish for a considerably brighter radiance.

The Christian will accept this humbling experience realistically as a matter of fact, even if he cannot entirely explain it and still less justify it in terms of cheap triumphalism (as it was called at the last general council). But, because a sincere Christian who acknowledges himself to be a poor sinner makes his own contribution to reducing the clarity of the Church's manifestation, he will certainly not pharisaically deduce from this lack of clarity a right to dissociate himself from this Church of sinners. Of course he always has a right to criticize. An ultimate identification with the fundamental nature of the Church—which it has not lost and never will lose—does not imply agreement with each and everything that is done in the Church. Not even with all that the hierarchy or the Pope does, nor with each and every item that is put forward as official teaching in the Church. For me the real dogma of the Church is an absolutely binding factor and as a Christian and as a theologian I have not infrequently had to make an effort to discover what was really meant by a particular statement put forward as a dogma by the Church's magisterium, in order to give my assent honestly and confidently. But I have never known an instance in the course of my life where it became impossible to give this assent; at least not when I had seen clearly that even these dogmas could all be understood rightly only as far as their meaning was related to the mystery of God himself, that they always appear in a form that is historically conditioned, are always and unavoidably blended with certain elements which do not properly belong to the content of what is said and can render the latter misleading, that these dogmas as formulated are partly linguistic rules which need not always take precisely this form to express the essential meaning.

It is however different in regard to the odd item of more or less secondary importance in the field of exegesis, systematic theology, moral theology, which has been or is put forward by the Roman magisterium as official and binding teaching, even though no definition is involved. To mention only recent *examples,* I do not see either in the arguments used or in the formal teaching authority of the Church as actually asserted a convincing or conclusive reason for assenting to the controversial teaching in Paul VI's *Humanae Vitae* or to the Declaration of the Congregation for the Doctrine of Faith which seems to exclude the ordination of women in principle and for all time. But the Church does not require from me such an identification with each and every declaration of the magisterium—apart from dogma properly so-called—either in practice or according to the principles related to this question as laid down in the normal course of its theology.

In this situation a Christian and a theologian need not feel that his attitude in dissociating himself from such teaching places him on the fringe of the Church. Things may not then always be too easy for him as a theologian. Even today objectively unjustified administrative measures are adopted which unduly restrict the theologian's legitimate freedom of opinion and research. But it is impossible to guard against such narrow-minded procedures from the outset in the Church as it actually exists, by facing the magisterium with the dilemma of proclaiming and protecting pure dogma alone *or* of remaining completely silent. All that is left to the theologian is to go as far as he can to ensure that blunders of this kind on the part of the official teaching authorities occur as rarely as possible, even though there is no *a priori* recipe for avoiding them all together; for the rest, he must patiently allow for such mistakes among the defects and sins that will never be lacking in the history of the Church of sinners. But in the last resort none of this disturbs the ecclesial allegiance of a Christian theologian in his actual existential relationship to the Church. I can understand that there are Christians who feel authorized or even bound in conscience to leave the Church exactly as I can recognize that many people can act with a clear conscience in the moral field in a way which my conscience would compel me to reject absolutely in practice and in principle. That is why I can still take for granted the ecclesial character of my being a Christian and of my theology.

This opportunity for a legitimate compromise arises of course most obviously in regard to participation in the life of the Church. If we examine them more closely, we can observe that the official norms for life in the Church, even in the Catholic Church, allow extraordinarily wide scope for diversities of organization. The house of the Church is much larger and for a long time has not merely consisted of tiny and stifling rooms. That is not to say that we should underestimate the importance, the religious strength and even a certain theological normative character of popular devotion, which is often much more noble, and understands more about God than anaemic rationalism or bourgeois respectability. But in 'our Father's house' there are many rooms among which we can and indeed must choose, if we want to justify our own life before God. At the same time we might wish that the Church's proclamation and its approved practice as expressed in the average sermon and in church newspapers would permit a little more of the spaciousness of the Church and the freedom of the Christian to be perceived. We cannot have a fatherland unless we are prepared to live with its philistines and slackers. It is the same with the Church. We must not simply identify the 'Catholicism' of a particular country with the Church as a whole and blame the latter for the narrowness and hard-heartedness of a particular regional Catholicism. But, even in a local church where this narrow-minded Catholicism prevails, the word of God and his grace is proclaimed, his forgiveness granted and the death and resurrection of Jesus celebrated until he returns.

It seems to me that those who suffer far too much through the Church have not properly understood its true nature and their ultimate relationship to it. If I live my Christianity quite naturally and without inhibitions, even somewhat casually as a result of habit, if I live it also within the Church, there can of course be moments when I am stirred into asking: 'What am I really doing here?' Then I tell myself (in regard to what is present even though inexpressible): 'You cannot flee to a greater clarity than what you have and you have no right to allow yourself, by attempting to take a more radical decision for your life, to fall into a greater darkness, simply because you could wish for a more radiant and compelling clarity than what you now possess.' I also tell myself: 'Accept the incomprehensible mystery with equanimity and serene hope; what then could go wrong?' What other choice could I make that was not long ago encompassed by this mystery? I tell myself: 'You will die and your death will strike at your whole existence and even the theory you have constructed about it; is it not pointless to do anything but die with Jesus into his death (and, consequently, to live now with him)?' I then tell myself: 'Is not this the sum-total of Christianity? Can we not simply accept everything else about Christianity, however difficult it is to understand and to bear, since it can only be had in its wholeness?' If I put these questions to myself and answer in this way, then it seems to me permissible to take my Christianity for granted, to think and to live the Incomprehensible very comprehensibly.[1]

---

[1] On all this cf. *Rechenschaft des Glaubens, Karl Rahner-Lesebuch,* ed. K. Lehmann and A. Raffelt (Freiburg/Zurich 1979). On Karl Rahner's status see especially A. Raffelt, 'Bibliographie der Sekundarliteratur', in H. Vorgrimler, ed., *Wagnis Theologie, Erfahrungen mit der Theologie Karl Rahner* (Freiburg 1979), pp. 598–622.

2

ON THE SITUATION OF FAITH

OUR THEME in the following reflections is faith: faith, that is, as understood by the magisterium of the Catholic Church and by traditional theology. Hence the author will not be disturbed by the objection that he is creating a lot of trouble and work for himself by discussing theologically a concept of faith that no longer corresponds to what people today and many modern theologians understand by the term.

What must be considered first of all in theological terms is the impossibility, only now becoming evident, of a positive integration of faith with the rest of what is known (at least by educated people and at least in the West). What do we mean in the first place by this impossibility of (reciprocal) integration? Because of the contingency of his history and because of the plurality of the sources of knowledge (beginning with the multiplicity of his senses), the diverse contents of a person's consciousness are not reciprocally integrated from the outset. Harmony does not prevail everywhere from the beginning. One of the main tasks of human knowledge as of *one* subject, despite the multiplicity of realities making up a human being, is to synthesize the many and at first sight very disparate experiences. Man strives for a completely structured world-view in which every object of his individual experiences has its definite place and in which all details are reciprocally explained and rendered intelligible, in which no contradictions appear. Because of the unity of consciousness and from the nature of the case it is necessary and understandable that the realities of his secular experience and those of the Christian faith should be integrated together into such a homogeneous world-vision.

The reality of faith is not simply a world to itself alone, separate from

13

the world of secular experience, if only because this faith raises quite concrete claims and demands which must be fulfilled in the concrete world of secular experience and activity, in moral life and in the ecclesial society, which is a very concrete reality of everyday existence. For this very reason the desire for a synthesis, for the integration of the reality of faith and of secular reality, must be recognized as legitimate in principle. The Christian rightly demands a homogeneous, completely structured 'world-view' in which his Christian faith properly so-called and the rest of his experience, the rest of his knowledge (including academic knowledge), are integrated. This 'world-view' is not simply present from the outset, otherwise the revelation of faith as such would have to supply also as its own content the totality of man's possible knowledge. But it does nothing of the kind, for revelation and Christian faith by their very nature exclude the possibility of such a homogeneous world-view present from the outset, arising out of the unity of the sources of knowledge.

Although man cannot live by faith alone (this essential limitation of revelation and faith is by no means obvious, but it is a fact), but can in fact live this faith only with the aid of the rest of his experience, a clearly and palpably completely structured world-view cannot exist from the outset: it must be sought and established, a task which for a Christian is a duty arising from his faith. Of course the task was accomplished at all times only as an asymptotic convergence toward the goal and, from the standpoint of the individual and his life-task, to be completed only in death. Nor of course was this task ever fully achieved even in a society. There were always elements of secular experience (in nature and history) not clearly synthesized with Christian faith or combined with the latter into a world-view, even though they had a certain relevance from the standpoint of faith. But in former times such relics of an experience subjectively already existing but not yet positively integrated into a homogeneous Christian world-view were comparatively slight, if only because people knew nothing at all about many secular facts relevant to faith but difficult to integrate. In Francis Suarez' world-vision, for instance, his faith with his theology and his secular knowledge of nature and history did not form an original unity from the outset, but they were easily and clearly visibly integrated into a unity. Everything fitted together and this harmony was not merely a fundamental postulate of his faith and of the original unity of his consciousness, but a perceptible fact.

Despite these elements of unresolved problems, in earlier Christian times there existed an assured, homogeneous world-vision, a completely structured world-view, which was not only that of the individual and the solitary isolated person on his own account and at his own risk, but that of a society where, despite individual heretics and dissidents, it was more or less taken for granted and undisputed, at least in its basic features. And, in so far as the fact was known existentially and taken seriously that there were and are also other religions and ideologies outside the Christian cultural complex, it was easily integrated into the Christian world-view by being explained in the light of data understood in Christian terms (original sin, culpable error, etc.) or by simply regarding supporters of these other religions and ideologies as enemies with whom from the outset there could be no dialogue, since the latter would constitute a threat to one's own world-view. At a still earlier stage these other ideologies were not regarded as unintegrated facts, threatening one's own world-view, but more or less as I might today regard a Tibetan medicine as irrelevant to my needs and leave it aside without trying to find out more about it. Of course, even in former times there were brief periods when a world-vision lost its clarity or disintegrated, periods also of struggle between several world-views. But such critical phases (for instance, the transition from the ancient 'pagan' world-vision to the Christian world-vision of the West) were comparatively brief, because a geographically restricted society, content through all the changes with its self-understanding, maintained a world-view which had its own unity and consistency.

It is different today, nor can it be foreseen how and when this new situation might change in the future, even though no one can say that this is simply impossible. There are two reasons why man today finds it impossible positively to integrate all the data of his consciousness with his faith. These are the extent of his secular knowledge and the necessity and real possibility of an existentially genuine dialogue with all existing forms of faith and ideologies.

First of all the present range of secular knowledge, as it exists or is in principle easily attainable for the individual, is so great that for him at least a positive synthesis with the Christian faith is concretely and practically impossible.

The abundance of knowledge yielded by the natural and historical sciences is so vast and increases so quickly that, even apart from faith, it can no longer be really synthesized in the head of any single individual. For the individual a system of knowledge into which new insights were slowly and cautiously integrated has now become an exploded chaos with which he cannot cope. Not only is there an endless number of things supposed to be 'known' today that he does not know, but as a matter of real and concrete experience he knows *that* he does not know all this. (This comes home to him particularly in the presence of a modern computer.) This is a quite different and new form of ignorance and it is accompanied by a feeling of helplessness and powerlessness which in former times would arise in face only of nature as a whole and not of human works.

This present and still unsurmounted mass of knowledge (always prior to any confrontation with faith) places man in a new and unique situation in regard to knowledge. Formerly there was an immense number of things that he did not know, but he was not aware or at the most only slightly aware of this ignorance existentially at the margin of consciousness. What was known was also known on the whole securely and without feeling threatened. Hence a person expressed his knowledge mainly in the form of a firm and more or less absolute statement of what he knew. Today the individual knows that a vast number of things of which he is ignorant is present all around him and that this number is speedily and enormously increasing, raising questions about the knowledge he already possesses as provisional and subject to revision. Consequently the individual today does not normally express his knowledge in the form of a firm statement, meant to be permanently certain and more or less absolute, but as provisional, open to question, hypothetical, valid for the time being; if further knowledge is acquired, this is seen only as superseding a hitherto accepted hypothesis. What results from all this is a diffuse but everywhere prevailing sceptical relativism. We no longer live in solid houses of absolutely sound convictions, accepted by society at large and everywhere taken for granted, but in tents hastily pitched for a journey into the unforeseeable, simply because we know so much and discover new things so quickly and each individual by himself becomes increasingly stupid in face of the range of what as such is immediately knowable or can be 'looked up', although technical inventions enable him to live continually with what he does not understand.

In his present state of knowledge the attitude of the individual to the Christian faith cannot simply be the same as formerly. A positive, uniform and clearly visible synthesis of this modern knowledge with faith to form a homogeneous world-view is not possible either objectively or subjectively. Christian faith can no longer be experienced so simply and obviously as formerly as the ultimate structural principle of knowledge as a whole. In principle at least, there does not seem to be any absolutely clear and as such certainly palpable contradiction between faith and modern knowledge, although psychologically and existentially it is not so simple to keep to the somewhat vague midway between the non-perceptibility of an absolute contradiction and the impossibility of seeing a positive reconciliation and synthesis between the two. But even if an absolute contradiction cannot be proved and if modern Christian apolo-getics is frequently content to restrict itself to this negatively protective defence, it must be clearly seen and carefully noted that for the individual such a positive synthesis between modern knowledge and ancient faith is largely impossible.

This needs to be elucidated in the light of individual, concrete exam-ples. We might be expected to produce examples of the impossibility of such a positive reconciliation between modern knowledge and Christian faith in the fields of both the natural sciences and the historical and social sciences. We might ask, for example, what an individual modern physi-cist is supposed to make of transubstantiation in the Tridentine teaching on the Eucharist. We might ask whether an individual historian of religion for his own part would also regard as certain the self-understand-ing of Jesus presented by traditional Catholic fundamental theology as historically certainly demonstrable. We might ask whether the historian or social scientist today can be so completely certain that Christianity (especially in the historical form of the Church) is palpably beyond comparison with other religions, as Vatican I declared it to be, claiming that this incomparability in terms of fundamental theology (that is, in historical empiricism) amounted to a comprehensible and conclusive argument for the supernatural origin of the Christian revelation, valid for all times and adapted to the intelligence of all. It might be asked what such present-day thinkers would make of the statements about miracles and even prophecies (tacitly passed over today, by contrast with Vatican I). It might be asked whether today they could without more ado regard the spread of the Church as miraculous, its moral state as one of out-standing holiness, its activity as inexhaustibly fruitful in all that is good, and thus see the Church itself—as Vatican I claimed—as an invincible testimony to its own divine mission.

We could go on at length in this way. It should not be maintained that there can be no appropriate suggestions or answers in regard to all these and many, many other questions. All that can be said here is that such answers, even if they are or can be assumed to be correct 'in themselves', do not make it any easier for the individual to integrate modern knowledge and Christian faith into a positively grasped unity of a world-view. No remedy has been found for this situation, no way of rendering such an integration possible. We must simply put up with this state of affairs, while showing that its real burden would not be removed from modern man even if he abandoned his faith and with that the possibility of the coexistence of Christian faith and modern knowledge. For the coexistence of convictions held as absolute and the immense number of opinions accepted only hypothetically and provisionally simply cannot be removed.

It is necessary now to consider more precisely the consequences for Christian faith as concretely lived, if it has to be lived in this atmosphere of sceptical relativism, of knowledge assumed to be provisional. The observations to be made here in response to the question are very unsystematic and are not meant to create an impression of being exhaustive.

First of all, the Church's teaching authority in practice and existentially takes a very secondary place in a person's 'system of faith' today. Of course it is part of the Catholic understanding of Christian faith to accept a magisterium which teaches with binding force. If this is *forthrightly rejected,* there can be no question of a truly Catholic understanding of faith. The authority of the Church and its magisterium however is certainly not the first and last foundation of the faith of a person today, but deduced as a very secondary factor, even though the latter—*if* and in so far as it is grasped by faith—helps to determine the faith of the individual Catholic in its totality. The teaching authority of the Church is certainly part of the substance of the Catholic faith, but, from the standpoint of fundamental theology, not its beginning nor its ultimate ground. Theoretically this had always been the position of Catholic fundamental theology, since it explained and justified its doctrine of the existence of God, of the possibility and reality of revelation, its doctrine of Jesus Christ as divine legate, *before* putting forward an ecclesiology, a doctrine of the Church's magisterium, of Scripture as inspired source of revelation. But in practice and kerygmatically, at an earlier stage, at least subliminally, a different mentality had existed. This was in line with Augustine's statement that he would not believe the gospel if he had not been moved to do so by the authority of the Church. In this view the Church, its authority, the stubborn absoluteness of its teaching, were regarded as the proper and sole refuge where people could be secure against their own scepticism and the breakdown of all certainties. From this standpoint they had an immediate and more or less natural understanding of the fact stressed (somewhat triumphalistically) by the Church that it was itself by its life and history an invincible motive of faith as a whole and not only a particular object of this faith with a relatively secondary place in its total structure and total justification.

Obviously there are many people even today who feel like this, because of their psychological make-up and sociological background. Here we shall not indulge in any prognosis as to whether this experience of the Church might not perhaps once again become generally the more or less obvious way of access to Christian faith as a whole. For it cannot at all be taken for granted that people must regard and will in future regard the sociological relativity of their convictions always as a reason for their uncertainty and not as a reason for their accuracy. But, granted all this and making allowance for it, it remains a fact that faith in the Church and particularly in its binding teaching authority is a conviction which today generally appears late and as a secondary element in the genesis and total structure of the Catholic faith. Man today is too well aware of the difficulty of deriving conclusions with logical necessity from the Church's history of dogma, as an explanation clearly emerging from the sense of faith of the primitive Church or even from the teaching of the historical Jesus. Even though this might be possible in theory, modern man as an individual cannot manage it; nor can he get very far by having recourse to the Church's authority in its present-day understanding of itself, since this very self-understanding appears as the result of a history the legitimacy of which he himself cannot clearly grasp. Man today has a different, prosaic and more or less demythologized attitude to authorities in general and to those who possess authority, since their history with its upheavals and mistakes is more obvious to him than it was to people in earlier times, and hence he knows also about the mistakes and wrong decisions in the history of the Church's magisterium.

The explanation that these mistakes—which cannot be denied—on the part of the Church's magisterium are involved in authentic doctrinal statements and not in definitions is of course objectively correct, but not easy for the individual to accept in practice today. For even statements that do not involve a definition can occasionally have very concrete and solid effects in the life of the Church and affect the individual very closely (we may recall, for example, *Humanae Vitae* or the Declaration on Women and the Priesthood). Moreover, in concrete cases, the Roman magisterium itself tends more to obscure than to clarify the difference between merely authentic statements and those involving a definition, thus creating the impression that it regards all doctrinal statements concretely and in practice as irreformable. But for this very reason the individual today is inclined to suspect that there is nothing to choose between statements involving a definition and merely authentic declarations of the magisterium. This impression is all the more widespread since the more simple Christian—not a professional theologian, but perhaps well-educated and even an 'intellectual'—often feels that modern theology puts forward interpretations even with reference to many dogmas that are so remote from the previous (popular) understanding that it is difficult for him to see how this new interpretation can be identified with the old dogma. In principle these interpretations can be necessary and legitimate today without posing a threat to the permanence of the old dogma. But the new interpretations make it more difficult for the individual Christian to adopt an unprejudiced attitude toward the Church's magisterium.

We shall not attempt here to deal further with the problems involved, still less to solve them. What should be noted here is that even existentially the Church's magisterium today is no longer the obvious starting point of faith, the obvious court of appeal which does not create any problems of its own, to which the preacher can have recourse; it is a comparatively secondary factor in the continually freshly realized genesis of faith, an object of proclamation and not the latter's essential foundation. Consequently, in proclaiming the Church's teaching on faith, the appeal to the authority of the magisterium must be handled very cautiously, particularly since it has also to be observed in this proclamation that the appeal to the sense of faith of the whole Church irrevocably upholding a particular doctrine (an appeal which even today still has an apologetic importance) and the appeal to the formal authority of the Roman magisterium are not precisely the same thing. Today this authority is in fact and in practice a permanent object of proclamation which must itself continually be made intelligible and credible in terms of fundamental theology and apologetics; it is not simply to be taken for granted everywhere and always as the ground of proclamation.

The further conclusion follows however that, if a particular dogma of the Church is to be made understandable and credible, the effort of proclamation cannot every time simply end with an appeal to the formal authority of the Church's magisterium: the dogma involved must be substantiated in terms of fundamental theology and apologetics in itself or in the light of more fundamental articles of Christian faith. This statement of course is a truism even for traditional fundamental theology. Hitherto however sermons generally started out too readily from the assumption that they took place within the dimension of the Church, the latter being regarded as an obvious and indisputable factor so that the sermon had only to be oriented to its teaching. Today even in the mystagogical sermon within the Church the person to be addressed is someone whose attitude to the magisterium and even to the sense of faith of the whole Church is not so ingenuous and naive as it was formerly. Proclamation within the Church must take the same form as outside it: in principle the dogmatic sermon must have an apologetic aspect; dogmatics and fundamental theology must mutually interpenetrate. Today no fundamental theology can exist or be presupposed in sermons which is assumed to have proved once and for all in a formal way the existence of a binding revelation, so that it can and must be asked only subsequently what in fact has been communicated by God in this revelation. Today it is the credibility (that is, the meaningfulness and existential assimilability and human unrenounceability) of the fundamental dogmas of Christianity that makes credible the existence of a supernatural revelation (rightly understood) and not *vice versa*.

The existence of the Church's magisterium and also its concrete importance as norm of faith for the individual may not be given up even today, but at the present time it has a different rank and a different place in the structure and in the 'system' of faith of a person today. The Church today—this may (and must, if the preacher is to be credible) be said without prejudice—is a burden: a burden which may not be thrown off, since that would be fatal in the long run to Christian faith (and recourse to the authority of Scripture alone also creates the same problems and difficulties in view of our present awareness of the historical relativity even of Scripture). But this burden must not be concealed, a person ought to feel the whole weight of the often terrifying history of the Church when the latter's authority is invoked; and it is only when the scandal of the cross—which is part of Christian faith—is honestly accepted without any triumphalism and preached in the same spirit that this burden can be turned into a blessing and the Church, despite everything, can be experienced as the obvious centre of faith, at which God's pledge of himself with irrevocable force in Jesus Christ is accepted.

We have to remember moreover a very different question with reference to the Christian faith which arises when we see this faith in the concrete human being in a situation which no longer permits a positive integration of faith and modern knowledge (in its own specific character). This situation poses a threat to that absolute assent which is part of the essence of Christian faith. The assent should be absolute, unconditional, firmer than anything else. As J. Beumer expresses it, the act of faith is 'by its nature a total surrender of man to God. But, in so far as this surrender is the free act of his knowledge precisely as response to God's word in revelation, it means certainty of faith. This implies (over and above the question of the relative certainty of the *praeambula fidei)** an absoluteness (firmness) of the 'decision for' (also as norm of knowledge) the object *(certitudo adhaesionis)* and of the (free) apprehension of the formal object of assent as such, absolutely and objectively guaranteeing the truth of the true and truthful testimony of God *(certitudo infallibilitatis),* so that the believer makes what is attested also epistemologically the absolute fixed point and the *norma non normata* of his knowledge' *(LThK* vol.iv, col.942). According to traditional teaching, then, faith is supposed to be absolutely and unconditionally the unambiguous first fixed point of all human convictions which (since God's truth has itself become its ground and formal object) is under no higher human authority, in the light of which it could be subjected to criticism and called in question. The problems involved in this doctrine of the certainty of faith, as they have always existed and for a long time been considered in traditional theology, and the diverse answers given in the traditional *analysis fidei,*† cannot directly concern us here but are presupposed as known.

The basic problem in this connection consists in the fact that this divine truth, which is supposed to guarantee the absolute certainty and firmness of faith, is always conveyed through human knowledge; the

---

* In traditional fundamental theology or apologetics the *praeambula fidei* included those truths, such as the existence of God, the possibility and historical fact of revelation, which could be shown to be accessible to reason, and the preliminary conditions—not the cause— of the assent of supernatural faith. Today these 'preliminaries' are seen to be more complex and less accessible to rational investigation, including psychological dispositions and openness to the workings of grace. Cf. Karl Rahner/Herbert Vorgrimler, 'Praeambula Fidei', in *Concise Theological Dictionary* (Freiburg/London 1965), pp. 368–70.—Translator.

† The analysis of the act of faith as discussed in the older manuals of dogmatics was intended to show how God could be directly attained only by faith, while faith itself is based on his authority as revealer. As with the *praeambula fidei* the problem is now seen to be more complex than formerly but also to be resolved only in the light of man's personal encounter with God in Christ. Cf. Rahner/Vorgrimler, *Concise Dictionary,* p. 19.—Translator.

question therefore arises why this human mediation with its dubiousness and uncertainty does not also affect the individual person's concrete faith, so that the latter cannot by any means have that certainty which the Church's teaching claims for it. Even though, as we said, we do not want to deal with this old and ever-new problem, it is obvious that the problem will take a different form and become more acute if the concrete situation in which God's absolute revelation to man must be conveyed in a human way is itself changed and becomes more critical.

In fact, in a mental climate in which in other matters the firm and indisputable statement (in any form and to any, albeit varied, extent) was the normal expression of human knowledge, the absolute assent of faith itself was not a particularly striking or unusual phenomenon in a person's consciousness as a whole. It appeared as a climax—not surprisingly —in a total system of securely, firmly and unchangeably maintained statements of a secular character. But, in a consciousness where a sceptical relativism normally prevails and all secular knowledge is regarded as merely provisional, to be superseded in the light of later experience, such an absolute assent of faith is bound to be seen as an alien element, as a demand which simply cannot be taken seriously by man today and which also shares in the changing, provisional and unforeseeable condition of all knowledge. In this situation the old problems of the *analysis fidei* acquire a wholly new importance and have consequences quite different from those of the past. Metaphorically speaking, when the king was an obvious, indisputable factor whose necessity in principle no critique would venture to question (at least not within the individual's sphere of existence), it was also easy to believe in the Pope; now that there are no more kings, belief in the Pope can no longer be taken for granted as it was formerly. Speaking without metaphors, formerly in the historical and sociological situation it was easier to perceive the certainty of the *praeambula fidei* and they posed no threat to faith itself, although of course it was even then clear that their certainty and the firmness of assent given to them were less than the certainty and firmness claimed by faith for itself. But today the concrete individual without a professional knowledge of theology, faced also with an abundance of historical and metaphysical problems beyond his control, unable to integrate modern knowledge and faith into a homogeneous world-vision, cannot be so certain as formerly of the *praeambula fidei* and this fact must also affect his faith. He feels insecure; he can no longer see clearly how to maintain the absoluteness and unconditional firmness of his faith.

Formerly, in the course of the analysis of the act of faith, it was easy to say that knowledge of the *praeambula fidei* was merely an external precondition of faith and, with its merely relative certainty, did not enter inwardly into faith and into its very structure, so that faith itself was determined only by its own internal formal object and was not affected by the relatively slight certainty of the *praeambula fidei* (the situation was said to be analogous to that of someone who gives absolute love and loyalty to a couple of human beings as his parents, although the certainty that these two really are his parents is not as absolute as his actual turning to them). But at that time the individual felt so certain about the *praeambula fidei* and took them so much for granted that he was easily satisfied with the explanation (in itself certainly theoretically correct) that the *praeambula fidei* (likewise certain and regarded as certain) did not enter at all into the inner nature of faith and were not themselves necessary to substantiate and justify the absoluteness of the assent of faith. But it is really not so simple today when the average person rightly or wrongly feels that his grasp of the *praeambula fidei* is much less secure or even non-existent. In practice and concretely this feeling is bound to be detrimental to the certainty of the assent of faith, whether this effect is logically necessary or not. For it is a question, not merely of the abstract nature of faith, but of its concrete existence in the consciousness of a person today, and this existence is undoubtedly also dependent on the existence and the specific character of the *praeambula fidei* at the present time in man's consciousness. He has the impression that for the time being he can believe to the best of his knowledge and in all conscience (in its actual state) in the same way as he finds it possible at the moment rationally to defend an opinion; he must however at the same time adopt the reservation, as with all other human knowledge, that he might later be better informed and then revise his previous view of faith; but there can be no talk of an absolute assent, excluding from the outset and in principle any later revision. We may well think that what has just been said expresses more or less accurately the present mentality in the western world, although of course the degree of explicit reflection on this epistemological situation of faith may vary considerably.

What however must be said of this imperilled state of faith in the light of faith's own understanding of itself? Can it exist also today with that absolute assent and that indisputable certainty which it formerly claimed for itself? Can the spiritual man judge everything while refusing to be judged himself, without making the hopeless attempt to escape from the mental climate of his time? What is to be said if we do not start out from the assumption that the traditional distinction between the rational grounds of assent to the *praeambula fidei* and the intrinsic formal object and motive of faith is a sufficient answer to our contemporary problem? If we attempt to give an answer to the question raised in this form, this does not mean that we regard the answer as exhaustive or that we might not bring in quite different considerations in order to find a comprehensive answer to our question.

In this connection it seems to me worth considering first of all that faith as *fides quae** is a many-sided factor. However much in itself and especially in the present mental climate it seems advisable and necessary to make clear the unity of faith, the internal connection of its individual statements, nevertheless the content of faith—particularly in the Church's official proclamation—is a many-sided and complex factor. Hence it can come about that a particular reality can actually be believed with a genuine theological faith, even though another part of the content of this same faith is simultaneously rejected as false. It can perhaps be said that someone who explicitly and publicly rejects a single dogma of the Catholic Church is a heretic and no longer belongs to that Church; but it cannot be said that the inculpable rejection of a certain dogma cannot coexist with a theological faith (as infused virtue and as act). For the Second Vatican Council declares that even a 'pagan' or an atheist, as long as he is true to his own conscience, can have a theological faith of the quality necessary for salvation.

If this is the situation, it is also conceivable that a Catholic Christian might not bring to certain dogmas of the Church that absolute assent which is part of the essence of faith and yet could be a believer in the theological sense of the term and also a Catholic, at least as long as he does not explicitly and publicly deny a particular dogma and as long as he remains in good faith. This is the position of many Catholics today. In the light of their mental attitude and psychological make-up, as these exist in the present age of sceptical relativism, despite their good will, they will not in fact succeed in bringing an absolute assent of faith to one dogma or another and yet it cannot be said on that account that they do not possess the faith necessary for salvation. The objection cannot be raised that such people are Catholics only if they affirm the Church and

* *Fides quae* = 'faith which (is believed)', the content of faith, as distinct from *fides qua* = 'faith by which (we believe)', the virtue of faith.—Translator.

its magisterium with an absolute assent of faith; if they do this, their absolute assent extends implicitly and necessarily to everything that the Church teaches with ultimate binding force; hence the situation described here simply could not arise for people who are Catholic and in practice lead a Christian life in the Church. This objection is not valid, since the statement that the Church is necessary for salvation and possesses an infallible magisterium, as a particular article of faith which entered comparatively late into the structure of faith, can itself be one of those articles to which a person inculpably fails to give an absolute assent of faith. It can be said then that, if there are very many people in the Church today who cannot manage a 'complete identification with the Church' (a favourite expression at the present time), if they give even to dogmas only that provisional and conditional assent which they give to statements of purely secular knowledge, if they live and 'practise' in this way in the Church, it cannot be simply claimed without more ado that they have no theological faith or do not belong to the Church.

Even a faith like this, still coming to be, not yet articulating certain elements of the one and entire faith with an absolute assent, can be an ecclesial faith leading to salvation. All that is required is that it does not imply an *absolute* rejection of a dogma of the Church. For the most part this will not happen today, since this modern man with his universal sceptical relativism (even in regard to his own opinions) will not be able or willing—even in regard to the Church's dogmas of faith—*absolutely* to reject a binding teaching of the Church merely because he cannot positively cope with it at the moment. If all this is true, then we can see quite dispassionately and in its concrete reality the faith of very many Catholics today and yet be optimistic about the salvation of this large number of Catholic Christians and about their attachment to the Church. Admittedly, they do not have the faith entirely as it is (rightly) described in the theological text-books; they do not say: 'I believe firmly and forever, with an irrevocable assent, everything that the Church teaches.' Or, if formularies of this kind are used at all, in practice these declarations are coloured by that sceptical relativism which affects all areas of consciousness today. Nevertheless, these people are Christians and Catholics.

This however is still far from being a sufficient answer to the question we raised. Is it possible to speak of a theological faith when there is nothing at all in the content of this 'faith' which is affirmed with an absolute assent of faith, when virtually everything that is 'believed' is accepted and lived only with that relativity and provisional character which are typical of the present time? Or in such a faith must there not be somewhere and somehow an absolute assent at least to certain articles without which the traditional teaching cannot conceive faith? Certainly justice is not done to the Church's teaching, the absolute importance of faith for a person who determines himself for his eternal destiny only by an absolute disposal of his freedom is not understood, if we purely and simply drop the whole idea of an absolute assent of faith. But where and how can a phenomenological description of faith today discover such an absolute assent among average human beings or even among ordinary Catholics? We could of course say that, because of the multiplicity of possible matters of faith, because of the plurality of human consciousness and the impossibility of adequate reflection, there is no difficulty in assuming that a Catholic who wants in principle to be a believer will somewhere and somehow come to a matter of faith which he grasps with an absolute assent, even though it is impossible to say precisely *what* is this matter of faith. This statement is certainly not simply false, but in itself it is an over-simplification. It is certainly possible to say something about this question without merely appealing to the fact that in the consciousness of a Christian attached to the Church there must inevitably be one thing or another that he apprehends with an absolute assent.

To get any further here, it must be remembered that man's freedom, in so far as it is not merely freedom of choice of a particular categorial object within the unrestricted range of consciousness, but the possibility of an inalienable disposal by the subject of itself as a whole in a basic decision, always exists absolutely in one way or another in the adult human being. In other words, man does not exist as a permanently neutral subject, doing one thing after another freely in a temporal succession, but as a subject which has decided about itself in a fundamental option (which of course does not mean that such a basic decision once made can never be changed). While it can always be revised, such an existential-personal decision is by its very nature an absolute decision in freedom and consequently the gnoseological element is also absolutely affirmed in it and yet this affirmation is free. Hence it cannot be said that for someone who has reached the use of reason and freedom absolutely everything in his consciousness is apprehended only conditionally and provisionally in knowledge and freedom. Even if this were so in the objectifying and verbalizing representational consciousness, even if a particular individual in his reflection were not able to apprehend something in his representational consciousness that he affirms as absolutely valid, if then in his reflective consciousness he were to mark every single objective reality of an external or internal character with the sign of sceptical relativism, none of this would prove that the free fundamental option in which the subject posits and understands himself is not an absolute assent in knowledge and freedom. At least the original protest of the subject against an absolute positing, the basic option for a universal sceptical relativism, would itself be an absolute positing. The necessity of an absolute decision is imposed on freedom, because the attempt at a universal abstention from such a decision in the concreteness of reality would itself be an absolute decision.

In the concrete order of reality however such a decision is always either belief or unbelief in the theological sense of the term. The freedom with which a person disposes of himself in a fundamental decision is the freedom of a subject with a 'supernatural existential', with an enduring actual offer of God, an offer presented to freedom as the innermost subjective principle of the orientation of men to the immediacy of God. The radicalizing of human transcendentality to the immediacy of God, which is involved in this continuous offering of supernatural grace, has the character of a revelation in the strictly theological sense of the term. If a person in his free, absolute self-understanding does not withdraw in culpable fear into his own finiteness but trustfully yields to the transcendentality of his mind oriented as it is to the incomprehensibility of God, he accepts himself in the transcendentality radicalized by grace to the immediacy of God: he believes and does so with an absolute assent. Even if someone tries to subject his representational and reflexive consciousness to a universal sceptical relativism, in the original, unreflecting realization of his freedom he is a believer or unbeliever with an absolute assent. Perhaps his inadequate means of reflection make it impossible for him to represent objectively the absoluteness of his fundamental option for belief or unbelief, but he does in fact believe or not believe, since a forthright existential abstention from a decision is impossible for the subject, placed as he is in his transcendental openness inescapably before God's gracious self-offering which he accepts or rejects.

Against this theory, which attempts to explain that even in face of a modern sceptical relativism an absolute assent of faith must be possible and does in fact occur, the objection might be raised that an absolute assent to a specific matter (or a particular aspect) of faith is not thereby made intelligible. *This,* it is claimed, is the kind of assent required by traditional theology when the latter speaks of an absolute assent of faith: it must be an assent to this or that in particular, 'something' must be believed and Christian faith must not (as it seems to be with Bultmann) be reduced to a formal *fides qua* without an assignable *fides quae*. But, according to this theory, the absolute assent remains restricted to the assumption of the subject's own objectless transcendentality, even though the latter is understood as radicalized by grace to the immediacy of God. What must be said with regard to this objection which creates the impression that the theory put forward dissolves Christian faith in a sublime existential ontology, since—according to this theory—what is in fact believed cannot be understood at all as coming from an historical revelation?

There is a great deal to be said in response to this objection. In the first place the assent of faith envisaged in this theory is clearly established by God's free self-communication to man's transcendentality. But where God's free action is involved, history in a sense—but in a true sense— exists, even though this free act of God does not take place at a definite point in place and time as part of the course of history, but is always and everywhere the condition—freely posited, but perceived as such—of the possibility of salvation history. The dilemma that something either fits *into* history at a definite and particular place and is therefore historical or is part of an 'essence' which as such is unhistorical, is false. Moreover, it must be said that the free acceptance of man's reference to God's immediacy, established by grace, normally takes place, not in an isolated mystical interiority, but—like everything pertaining to man's transcendentality—is brought about by the encounter with an *a posteriori* 'objective reality' in other persons or in the environment. By his concrete encounter with his historical world a person becomes aware of himself and thus also of his transcendentality to God in himself radicalized by grace. This mediating historical reality as such does not itself necessarily have the character of being revealed in the strictly theological sense; in itself it can be secular and worldly, as long as it is assumed that it can mediate an act in which the subject really disposes of himself in freedom and accepts himself as he is: that is, also (implicitly) with its reference by grace to God.

Expressed in scholastic terminology: in the present order of salvation, in which by God's offer of himself man is ultimately referred always and everywhere to God's immediacy, it follows that every *actus honestus* is also in practice an *actus salutaris,* even if this act is not expressly con-

cerned with a revealed reality and motivation of an objective and verbalized nature (to deny this would be to contradict Vatican II, according
to which even an atheist or a 'pagan' can posit a salutary act of faith).
Such an objective reality, which has a moral significance and (at least
implicitly) is in any case covered by the 'authority' of God (which indeed
is an essential aspect of an *actus honestus),* can however be regarded in
an adequate sense as a categorial object of revelation, even though it is
not 'revealed' as such for its own sake nor (to express it better and more
precisely) presented in this sense for our reflection. For it is certainly
possible to deny at once that there is a *moral* object for an *actus honestus*
which is not *also* revealed as such (however theology may explain more
precisely the revealed character of matters that are already part of the
natural moral law). But if the object of an *actus honestus* does not lie
purely and simply outside the dimension of revelation and (this must not
be overlooked) is grasped in the subject's mental activity as a whole,
radicalized by grace and consequently no longer simply 'natural', then
it can confidently be maintained that such a mediation to itself of the
subject elevated by grace is to an adequate degree an object of revelation:
that is, not only the *fides qua* but also the *fides quae* belonging to the
sphere of revelation. These problems could perhaps be given a better and
clearer treatment than has been attempted here. But they are problems
not only arising from the thesis that an absolute assent is possible for
every human being who is not culpably an unbeliever and that it exists
even in today's mental climate of sceptical relativism, but also imposed
on every theologian who does not reject Vatican II's optimism in regard
to salvation, who does not deny the possibility of a really salvific faith
even on the part of someone who in his reflection inculpably regards
himself as a 'pagan' or atheist.

It may be said then that there will be many Christians and Catholics
today who include at least in their reflective consciousness many individual dogmas of Christianity to which they do not give an absolute
assent or which they even reject 'conjecturally'—reacting, that is, in a
spirit of sceptical relativism—and thus very often finding themselves
facing the question of whether they are still Christians and Catholics.
From what has been said up to now it is possible to answer this last
question in the affirmative, since even with such people there is or can
be an absolute assent, since the 'rejection' of particular dogmas does not
take the form of absolute unbelief in a theological sense: it is not really
a public repudiation in the sight of the Church.

It is from this standpoint that the question should be considered more closely in practical theology as to how such Christians and Catholics are to be treated in the course of concrete pastoral activity. They are often called 'marginal Catholics' as if theirs was a perfectly simple albeit very unstable relationship to the Church. From what has been said it should really be clear that this view is not as unproblematical as it is often assumed to be in the pastoral care of these people. The essential theological problem for practical theology does not lie in the simple fact that this is the state of the faith of some Catholics and is tacitly accepted and tolerated (which is what largely happens), but in the fact that they may be told to stay like that for the time being , so that they do not simply and completely turn their backs on the Church. An educated Catholic might be addressed, for instance, in this way:'If you think you don't understand some particular dogma, that you can't grasp it inwardly, that you can't believe it, you should not say that the dogma is false, absurd and must simply be rejected; this does not fit in with your general mental attitude, your fundamental sceptical relativism. Don't get on your high horse as if you were a professional theologian making a final, academic decision about a particular question of theology. You would not deal with other metaphysical questions in that way. If on the other hand you affirm the ultimate basic substance of Christianity, the existence of God, a prayerful relationship to him, an ultimate trust in Jesus as the unsurpassable self-promise of God to you, if you practise also a religious life in the Church so far as this is declared by the Church to be really indispensable—and, if we look at it more closely, not very much is required—then you need not hesitate to regard yourself as a Catholic and you can confidently leave to the future the further development of your religious life, for which you want to remain open; you have no reason to think that intellectual honesty requires you to leave the Church.'

There is no doubt that some people are inclined as representatives of the Church to speak in this way to 'educated' Catholics at the present time. It should be clear from our reflections that it is *permissible* to speak in this way (with discretion of course and in a form adapted to the concrete case). At the same time (this must be stated explicitly once more) the dogma of the Church's teaching authority is not a special case for which an exception should be made. For precisely this absolute teaching authority of the Church is one of the dogmas which, despite its truth, a person today will find difficult to accept with an absolute assent of faith. And what has been said of the Church's dogma in general is true also of this particular dogma. If such a dogma is not (yet) accepted with an absolute assent of faith, there can nevertheless be a faith in the form of an absolute assent (under given circumstances) in the theological and ecclesial sense. This is a thesis which may lead to the frontier between ecclesial and non-ecclesial Christians becoming somewhat less clear than had hitherto been the case. But for the Church's pastoral practice this frontier—although rarely considered as such—was always very vague and fluid. The thesis put forward here really does not change anything of this. All it does (and this is important) is to make possible an approach with a clear and secure theological conscience to very many modern Christians as they really are, to justify an attitude of frankness and sympathy towards such people. It is an attitude often adopted in practice, but it should also be based on a clear conscience.

PART TWO

Priesthood

3

WOMEN AND THE PRIESTHOOD

O N 15 October 1976 the Sacred Congregation for the Doctrine of the Faith published with the approval of Pope Paul VI a 'Declaration on the Question of the Admission of Women to the Ministerial Priesthood'. In what follows we shall put forward some theological reflections on this declaration. These—if only because of the limits of space on the one hand and the vast range of the theme on the other—will be restricted to the properly theological aspect of the question involved and in fact to the theological aspect of *this* declaration, not to all the theological problems raised by the question of the possibility or non-possibility of the ordination of women as such. This restriction must be noted from the very outset. Consequently a number of questions are excluded which could be and perhaps ought to be raised in connection with our theme: questions emerging from a secular anthropology of the sexes, from the history of civilization, from an analysis of modern society with its demand for equality of the sexes, and so on. Neither are we dealing with all the present-day problems of pastoral theology which make the question of the admission of women to the priestly ministry relevant in quite a new way. If then we limit our reflections to the strictly theological aspect—that is, to the question as to whether it is certain that the Christian revelation in its unchangeable substance excludes women from the priestly ministry in the Catholic Church—we shall be able to avoid those emotions which so much affect the public debate on one side or another.

THE DECLARATION OF THE CONGREGATION FOR THE
DOCTRINE OF THE FAITH OF 15 OCTOBER 1976

The Declaration of the Congregation for the Doctrine of the Faith,
which takes up fifteen pages in the official translation,* begins within an
introduction on the role of women in modern society and in the Church
and is then divided into six parts. The first part refers to the 'constant
tradition' which always and everywhere in the whole course of Church
history (apart from some heretical sects) indisputably and uniformly
excluded women from the priestly ministry, so that the magisterium
never needed to intervene to reinforce a principle and a law which had
never been questioned. In the second part the attitude of Christ is examined and it is pointed out that he did not call any woman 'to become part
of the Twelve', although his attitude to women otherwise was quite
different from that of his milieu and represents a deliberate and coura-
geous break with it. The conclusion is drawn that Jesus intended in
principle to exclude women from the priestly ministry for all times and
under all sociological conditions, although it is admitted that a purely
historical exegesis of the texts of Scripture does not 'make the matter
immediately obvious'.

In a third section the Declaration refers to the practice of the Apostles
who had a higher appreciation of women than Jewish customs suggested
and were aware of emancipatory trends in the Hellenistic world. Yet they
never thought of conferring ordination on women, since they were convinced of their duty of fidelity to the Lord on this point. In a fourth
section of the Declaration the permanent value of the attitude of Jesus
and the Apostles is stressed. It is said that their attitude cannot be shown
to have been inspired solely by social and cultural motives, since in fact
they disregarded these when they rose above the discriminations practised against women at the time. It is then also pointed out that the
Church certainly has power over the sacraments with reference to the
exact shaping of the outward sign and the details of their administration,
but has no power over the substance of the sacraments. At the end of
a none too lucid argument the conclusion is then drawn that the
Church's practice of excluding women from the priesthood has a normative character. In any case therefore the Church's power over the sacra-

* English translation by Catholic Truth Society (London 1976), Do. 493.

ments cannot be used as an argument for admitting women to the priesthood.

In the fifth and sixth parts the priesthood is considered in the light of the mystery of Christ and the Church in order to clarify with the aid of the 'analogy of faith' the conclusions reached in the first four parts. Since at the same time it is expressly observed that these reflections do not present a conclusive argument, but since their conclusions are apparent only to someone already convinced by the reasons actually invoked while making a very speculative impression on others, even though these sections occupy a comparatively large part of the Declaration, there is no need to refer to them at length in the present article. For reasons of space, therefore, we shall leave them aside in the course of our further reflections, while admitting of course that they very often provoke counterquestions and opposition.

THE THEOLOGICAL QUALIFICATION OF THE ROMAN DECLARATION

If a theologian seeking a strictly theological statement of the question does not approach the basic content of the Declaration from the outset with an unambiguously preconceived opinion or with strong but understandable feeling, if he is ready to respect in principle the teaching authority of the Congregation for the Doctrine of the Faith, he will first of all raise the question of the theological qualification of the Declaration. The answer must be given straightforwardly and without prejudice that it is an authentic declaration of the Roman authorities on faith. Such a declaration obviously carries a certain weight merely in virtue of the formal authority of the Roman magisterium, independently of the arguments put forward by that authority; it cannot be judged by a theologian simply as a statement by some other theologian, the importance of which would be no more than the importance of the arguments put forward. Nevertheless, despite papal approval, the Declaration is not a definitive decision; it is in principle reformable and it can (that is not to say *a priori* that it must) be erroneous.

If the Declaration appeals to an uninterrupted tradition, this appeal is not necessarily and justifiably an appeal to an absolutely and definitively binding tradition, an appeal to a tradition which simply presents and transmits a 'divine' revelation in the strict sense, since there is obviously a purely human tradition in the Church which offers no guarantee of truth even if it has long been undisputed and taken for granted. With this Declaration, which has an authentic but not defining character, the fundamental question is whether the appeal is to a 'divine' or a merely human tradition. The decision itself of course seems to imply the former, but does not make this absolutely clear, particularly since it is admitted that hitherto the undisputed practice did not call for any more precise and closer reflection: that is, there has been scarcely any reflection on the precise nature of this tradition in actual practice.

We are then, dealing here, with an authentic but in principle reformable declaration from which error is not certainly *a priori* excluded and not with a simple reference to an absolutely certain doctrine of faith which is clearly and irreformably binding for other reasons. What should be the attitude of the theologian and believer to such an authentic but in principle reformable declaration of the Roman magisterium is perhaps expressed most clearly in the letter of the German bishops on 22 September 1967 to all those charged by the Church with the proclamation of the faith, which need not be quoted at length here.[1] This instruction speaks unashamedly of the fact that 'errors can occur and have occurred in the exercise of the Church's teaching authority', that the Church has always been aware of this possibility, says so in its theology and has worked out rules for dealing with the situation.

The situation of the theologian with regard to the theological qualification of the Roman Declaration in question is not a simple one. He must bring to such a decree the respect it deserves; nevertheless he has not only the right but also the duty of examining it critically and under certain circumstances of contradicting it. The theologian respects this decree by attempting to appreciate as impartially as possible the reasons it puts forward, by respecting as a matter of course the consequent practice of the Church as binding for him (at least for the present), by seeing as reinforced by the decree the conclusion that the general awareness of the Church in regard to the legitimate opportunities of women in the Church as a whole has not yet reached the point at which we could speak of a general change of awareness.

The theologian however has also the right and duty of critically examining this Roman Declaration, even to the point of regarding it as objectively erroneous in its basic thesis. In the nineteenth and twentieth

---

[1] Cf. J.Neuner/H.Roos, *Der Glaube in den Urkunden der Lehrverkündigung* (1971), nn.468–69.

centuries (to say nothing at all about earlier times) there is a whole series of declarations of the Roman authorities on faith which have meanwhile been shown to be erroneous or at least largely obsolete. Such progress in knowledge is absolutely necessary for the effectiveness of the Church's proclamation and simply cannot be conceived in practice without this sort of critical co-operation on the part of the theologians. It might indeed be said that such processes of revision have frequently taken too slow a course during the past hundred and fifty years, to the detriment of the Church, because theologians exercised their indispensable function too nervously and under the threat of the Church's disciplinary measures. With the increasingly rapid development and change of awareness in secular society today, these processes of revision can sometimes become more urgent and require more than formerly the honest and sincere work of theologians, even if this is wearisome and can at first expect little gratitude or recognition on the part of the Roman magisterium.

OBSERVATIONS ON THE ARGUMENTATION

In these circumstances the theologian has the right and duty to examine the arguments contained in the decree and to assume that, if this examination produces a negative result, the basic thesis of the Roman Declaration can itself be questioned and even be impugned as erroneous. What then is the value of the arguments put forward in the second to the fourth section of the Roman Declaration? (As we said earlier, we are leaving aside the fifth and sixth sections of the Declaration, since this argument from the 'analogy of faith' is admitted there to be convincing only to someone who has accepted the basic thesis in virtue of the arguments in the second to the fourth section.) The essential argument of the Declaration takes the line that the practice of Jesus and the Apostles, which makes no suggestion of the ordination of women to the priesthood, cannot be explained in the light of the sociological and cultural situation at the time and therefore assumes an intention on the part of Jesus which is not historically and sociologically conditioned: that is, it holds for all times and must be respected faithfully by the Church at all times. This argument is clarified by a reference to the fact that Jesus (and, up to a point, also Paul) in his sociological and religious appraisal of women took up a position completely opposed to the depreciation of women at the time and thus could have spoken out against the exclusion of women from positions of leadership in a secular or religious community, if he too had regarded this exclusion as caused merely by the sociological situation at the time. What must be said about these arguments?

Before reaching the crucial point of our own opinion after a proper critique of this argumentation, here are some brief preliminary observations. In the entire course of the argumentation it is never made sufficiently clear on whom the burden of proof really lies in the whole controversy. If the Declaration says, for example, that the opposite thesis is not and cannot be proved, it shifts the real burden of proof to its opponents. But is this really justified as long as the basic thesis of the Declaration has not been established as certain or (in other words) when at least the possibility must be envisaged of explaining the practice of Jesus and the Apostles simply by the sociological and cultural conditions of their time, particularly since the Declaration admits that some of Paul's ordinances on the behaviour of women are influenced by 'the customs of the period' and therefore 'no longer have a normative value'?

The argumentation of the Declaration is defective also in other ways. Thus the transition from the concept of the apostle and the Twelve to the concept of the priest (and bishop) in the Declaration is too simple to fit in with our present-day knowledge of the origins, structure and organization of the primitive Church. If we appreciate the difficulties created by these discoveries, which cannot be ignored, we may wonder whether it is possible to deduce from Jesus' choice of men for the college of the Twelve any definite and unambiguous conclusions with regard to the question of an ordinary, simple leader of the community and president of the eucharistic celebration in a particular congregation of a later period. The Declaration leaves out all the difficult questions about the concrete emergence of the Church and its origin from Jesus, although they are of the greatest importance for its theme.

It might also be asked whether, in view of the cultural and sociological situation at the time on the one hand and the 'immediate expectation' (generally admitted today as a fact) on the other, it is possible to look at all to Jesus and the Apostles for a plan in regard to the structure of the communities which (over and above what might be deduced for the Church from the event of salvation in Jesus' death and resurrection) could really be related to later times unambiguously and for ever.

Nor does the Declaration make use of a clear and comprehensive concept of the priestly ministry. In the fifth and sixth sections especially the proper function of the priest seems to be restricted more or less to the sacramental power of consecration, so that we almost get the impression that the Declaration would be prepared to concede to women practically all ecclesiastical functions except this one (and 'the official and public proclamation of the message', which hardly seems consistent with Jesus' commission to the women—mentioned in the second section—'to take the first paschal message to the Apostles themselves'). But there can be no doubt that such a narrowing down of the concept of 'priest' must rouse very serious dogmatic and particularly pastoral misgivings.

The Declaration admits that its arguments 'do not make the matter immediately obvious'. If it has been established that a particular statement is indeed part of the content of revelation, we certainly cannot expect the arguments to make this 'immediately obvious'. But what is the situation if such a statement has not been proved to be certainly contained in revelation, if in particular the question persists as to whether a long and undisputed practice of the Church (and the teaching implied in it) rests on a truly divine revelation or represents merely a human tradition, which can also exist for a long time and be undisputed in the Church and yet need not be revealed and can even be erroneous or possess no permanent normative value? In such cases it cannot simply be maintained that a theological argument does not need to be immediately obvious from the historical exegesis of the texts, even if it is admitted that the term 'obvious' is very ambiguous and that there are many varieties and degrees of 'obviousness'.

WAS THE ATTITUDE OF JESUS AND THE APOSTLES CULTURALLY AND SOCIOLOGICALLY CONDITIONED?

We come finally to the crucial point in the argumentation of the Roman Declaration. Once more a preliminary observation must be made. A practical rule of action can be culturally and sociologically conditioned and be open to change and actually changed as a result of a changed cultural and sociological situation and yet at an earlier stage may not only have existed and been sociologically recognized, but may even have been morally binding. Such a situation and the rules derived from it may have been 'objectively' opposed to more general and more fundamental moral principles also recognized and affirmed at the time, but not then seen or only slowly seen clearly as opposed in the consciousness of a society. As a result the more general principle only slowly changed the situation in that society and made it aware of a new and more concrete rule of action, although previously a contrary concrete rule not only existed in fact but was at the time morally permitted or even binding, since it was impossible or only possible by immoral violence to change the sociological situation from which it had emerged.

This fundamental consideration certainly does not need to be supported by examples or substantiated in principle. If someone wants examples, he has only to recall the institution of slavery during the first Christian centuries, polygamy in the Old Testament, the laws of war in the Old Testament, or the Church's prohibition of usury until well into the eighteenth century. In all these cases it is decisively important to observe that a concrete rule of action coexisted with more general moral principles, while being really 'in the abstract' opposed to the latter, although this basic contradiction could not in practice be perceived in the earlier sociological situation. Hence this particular rule of action could be permitted, *rebus sic stantibus,* and even be required, thus slowing down change in the situation on which it depended.

If we keep in mind these assumptions—obvious enough in themselves —then we can say confidently and with adequately certain historical knowledge that in the cultural and sociological situation at the time Jesus and the early Church could not in practice have considered and still less set up any female congregational leaders or presidents of the eucharistic celebration; their procedure could even have been morally required in the light of the existing concrete situation; in their concrete situation they simply did not need to observe and could not have observed a contradiction 'as such' and in the abstract between their general appreciation of woman (in which they dissociated themselves from the mentality of their time) and their concrete practice with the concrete rules that this implied, any more than Jesus or Paul could have been expected to notice explicitly the contradiction between their fundamental appreciation of human dignity and the acceptance of slavery as it existed at the time and still less to attempt expressly to oppose and to abolish this slavery.

The practical existence of a situation causing and explaining all this is not disproved by pointing to the fact that even under these conditions there were marginal phenomena which were really opposed to the cultural and sociological situation as a whole, since such unnoticed and in the last resort unnoticeable contradictions are an essential part of human existence and of the continual change in the course of history. But

Judaism in Jesus' time (as is clearly noticeable still in Paul's writings) was based on a male domination so much taken for granted that it is quite impossible to think that Jesus and his Apostles (and with them their Hellenistic congregations under the influence of Judaism) could have abolished or even have been permitted to abolish this male preponderance in their congregations, despite the more fundamental and more general recognition of the equal dignity and equal rights of women which they themselves were bringing about in the religious sphere and—up to a point—even within the dimension of secular society.

At the same time the fact should not be overlooked that, if its basic thesis is not assumed as *a priori* certain, the burden of proof evidently lies with the Declaration and not with its opponents. In any case the cultural and sociological situation with regard to the position of women at the time of Jesus was such that there would have been considerable resistance (if nothing more) to the appointment of women as leaders in the congregations. At the same time the question must be considered from the standpoint of leadership in the congregation and not from that of strictly sacramental powers, if we are not *a priori* to interpret the primitive Church quite unhistorically while overlooking the fact that there is no immediate evidence of a special power over the Eucharist anywhere in the New Testament. If then in any case there are cultural and sociological reasons for not making a woman leader of the congregation, it ought to be clearly proved that these reasons are not of themselves sufficient to explain the attitude of Jesus and the Apostles. But the Declaration makes no attempt to provide such a proof.

Moreover, if it is assumed that Jesus and the Apostles had different and more substantial reasons for their action than the existing cultural and sociological situation, then it should be explained more precisely and in detail in what these other reasons consist; otherwise their attitude would appear to be based on an arbitrary decision. But in this respect too the Declaration is completely silent. The mere fact that Jesus was of the male sex is no answer here, since it is not clear that a person acting with Christ's mandate and in that sense (but not otherwise) *in persona Christi* must at the same time represent Christ precisely in his *maleness*. But if we were to appeal to the 'divine order of creation' in order to find and try to develop such reasons, then it would certainly be difficult (as is evident from the mistaken arguments of the Fathers of the Church and the medieval theologians) to avoid appealing to an anthropology which would again threaten what the Declaration recognizes as the equal dignity and equal rights of woman.

It is not possible at this point to set out in detail the historical material explaining why Jesus and the Apostles in their concrete cultural and sociological milieu could not (without attempting what was impossible at the time) have thought of appointing women to be properly speaking leaders of the congregation or to preside at the Eucharist or even why nothing of this kind could have emerged in that situation as a serious possibility; why the assumption of such an outlook on their part would be like expecting them expressly to oppose the institution of slavery at the time or at least to abolish it among Christians, merely because they were convinced of the fundamental equality and dignity of all men. For the historical material in general the reader must be referred to the specialist works of reference. For the non-specialist the material (including additional literature) presented and evaluated by Haye van der Meer in his book *Priestertum der Frau?*[2] is still adequate.

If in scrutinizing and evaluating this historical material we must differentiate between the Jewish and the Hellenistic milieu (on which the Declaration insists), this distinction in the last resort is of little importance for our question, since the structure of a Hellenistic Christian community was considerably influenced by primitive Jewish Christianity and since there was serious discrimination against women also in the Hellenistic milieu; the existence of priestesses in some of the cults of pagan deities (cults which were deeply loathed anyway by Christians under the influence of Judaism) made no difference to this. What otherwise is the explanation of the fact that the Fathers of the Church (and also the medieval theologians) under the influence of Hellenistic society and philosophy enormously depreciated woman—as the Declaration itself admits, albeit somewhat tentatively—and that they brought forward largely these (and not other) reasons against the admission of women to the priesthood, if they had other and better reasons based on the gospel? Once again the historical material will not and cannot be set out here.

If however the assumptions stated above and the methical considerations likewise merely indicated can be recognized, then the conclusion seems inescapable that the attitude of Jesus and his Apostles is sufficient-

[2] Freiburg 1969. ET: *Women Priests in the Catholic Church? A Theological-Historical Investigation,* trans. Leonard Swidler and Arlene Swidler (Philadelphia 1973).

ly explained by the cultural and sociological milieu in which they acted
and had to act as they did, while their behaviour did not need to have
a normative significance for all times—that is, for the time when this
cultural and social milieu had been substantially changed. It does not
seem to be proved that the actual behaviour of Jesus and the Apostles
implies a norm of divine revelation in the strict sense of the term. This
practice (even if it existed for a long time and without being questioned)
can certainly be understood as 'human' tradition like other traditions in
the Church which were once unquestioned, had existed for a long time
and nevertheless became obsolete as a result of a sociological and cultural
change,

THE DISCUSSION MUST CONTINUE

The theologian is now faced with a Declaration of the Roman magisterium, authentic but open to revision and reform, which he must treat with
respect while having the right and duty to consider it critically. To some
theologians at least and perhaps to many such a critical examination
seems to show that the arguments of the Declaration are not adequate.
Hence all that we can say is that the discussion may and must continue
on the problem at issue even after this Declaration; the discussion is not
yet at an end and it cannot consist merely in a defence of the basic thesis
and arguments of the Declaration. If this is the state of affairs, then the
discussion must no longer be centred merely on the dogmatic question
in the strict sense, whether in the attitude of Jesus and the Apostles there
is or is not implied a doctrine of revelation properly so called.

The discussion must and can be extended again to all the aspects and
questions which have been more explicitly or freshly involved in the
theological discussion of the last decades. These include questions about
the sociological emancipation of woman in theory and practice, questions about the consequences of woman's sociological emancipation in
the life of the Church (questions which are there anyway), questions
about overcoming discrimination against women in the Church (a discrimination which is still far from being eliminated, even if we disregard
our main theme); questions about the authentic and integral essential
image of the priest, which cannot be restricted to his purely sacramental
power; questions about present-day requirements for the structure of a
Christian congregation and about the function of women in the Church

as determined by that structure; questions about the concrete methods and measures by which the discrimination against women in Church and society persisting before and after merely theoretical ideals can be effectively overcome in life and in society and about the different requirements in different cultural groups; questions about ways and means of educating and changing the consciousness of the Church as a whole, where the causes of such a change of consciousness are to be found and what are the factors preventing it, how and in what form due consideration can and must be given—in accordance with Paul's teaching—to the 'weakness' of this consciousness in many members and parts of the Church (a matter which is of great importance also for our main question); questions of principle finally about methods, how in fact the essential problem that occupies us here must be realistically tackled and surmounted (questions which are still far from finding a clear and generally accepted solution in detail, since we really have no clear answer, for example, to the problem of how to distinguish in principle between a 'divine' tradition and a generally and long-enduring 'human' tradition).

Our main problem ought to be set against the background of all the questions and of the answers to them, if we are to hope for an answer to it in the foreseeable future: an answer on which believers in the Church and the magisterium in Rome can be in complete agreement in theory and practice. Despite its argumentation, theology also is always and simply cannot fail to be historically conditioned and dependent on the pre-scientific milieu, on cultural and sociological preconceptions, attitudes and experiences of life, on the ethos of a society and its life-style. These assumptions can sometimes be very variable, but cannot be changed merely by theoretical scientific reflection, but in the last resort only by life and history in freedom, action and decision.

If in this way the total situation of woman in the society and also in the Church of the immediate future is everywhere further changed, if defenders and opponents of the Declaration work for it, since such a common effort is possible and necessary and since the still persisting discriminations against women in the Church are admitted by both sides, then the common effort can bring about that cultural and religious situation in which the problem of the Declaration still remaining but at present insoluble in practice in the Church can be left to await a solution acceptable *to all sides*. In other words, when woman has acquired practically and institutionally in the Church that importance which as such she ought to have, which this Declaration also concedes to her in practice but which in fact she does not yet possess, then only are the vital presuppositions present for a solution satisfying to all sides of the main problem which occupied us here. Then we can and must wait patiently to see how the solution turns out.

This of course is not to say that until then a moratorium must be declared in theology. Theology ought even now to continue its reflections, since this effort too can and must help to bring about that mental and religious outlook which is a necessary presupposition of a generally accepted solution of the problem. The opponents of the Roman Declaration will of course even now think and hope that a development will lead to a clarification of the Church's sense of faith which will prove them right; they will regard such a development as analogous to that which led from Gregory XVI and from Pius IX's Syllabus to the Pastoral Constitution *Gaudium et Spes* and the Declaration on Religious Freedom at the last council. But, as we said, we can wait for all this with patience and confidence. Nevertheless, too many demands must not be imposed on this patience, for time presses and we cannot wait again for a hundred years for an analogous development without detriment to the Church.

The Roman Declaration says that in this question the Church must remain faithful to Jesus Christ. This is of course true in principle. But what fidelity means in connection with this problem remains an open question. Consequently the discussion must continue. Cautiously, with mutual respect, critical of bad arguments on both sides, critical of irrelevant emotionalism expressly or tacitly influencing both sides, but also with that courage for historical change which is part of the fidelity which the Church owes to its Lord.

PART THREE

Life in the Church

4

THE CHURCH'S RESPONSIBILITY
FOR THE FREEDOM OF THE INDIVIDUAL

S O MANY obscure questions are implicit in this theme, its scope as such is so wide, that I must from the outset issue a warning and offer an apology for the fact that my treatment of it is very fragmentary and my selection of the points it offers for reflection and discussion very arbitrary. For what is freedom? Does anything like this exist at all? Is freedom not a lovely mirage hovering behind genetic, psychological and sociological determinisms and constraints? How are we to define philosophically the concept of freedom? How are we to make clear the transcendental necessity compelling man, despite the sheer factuality of his existence, to see himself as a subject of freedom, even though his reflection never enables him adequately to distinguish in his concrete action between the consequences of the factors determining his existence and the inescapable and inalienable consequences of his freedom. What are we supposed to be talking about when we use this term 'freedom'? About freedom and the scope for freedom in a society, despite and as opposed to its power-structures, freedom of the subject as such against internal constraints and overpowering forces in his own nature with all its strata, the unity and distinction between these two freedoms? What is meant by that freedom in Paul's sense which is the essence and peculiarity of redemption, justification and grace? What is the relationship of this freedom as eschatological possession of salvation to man's freedoms from internal and external constraints and from alienations? What is the relationship between the will and hope for eschatological freedom, which is ultimately God's gift, and the will and hope for a greater socio-political freedom?

What has the Church to do with all this? Is it the mediator of that

51

eschatological freedom which comes from God in the liberation by grace from all 'authorities and powers' enslaving man externally and, even more, internally? Has the Church—which of course is also a society—from its very nature a mandate to promote greater freedom within itself?[1] Is it not itself also continually in danger of becoming enslaved to that very thing which it is its proper mandate to oppose. Why in its proclamation and theology is there so comparatively little talk of *that* freedom which is notably at the heart of Pauline teaching on salvation? Why is the proclamation of the law so far from being clearly the proclamation of the freedom of the Christian, aware in his immediacy to God of only one 'law': that is, the law of freedom in the Spirit of God himself who is love? What is the Church's task in regard to all the aspirations and struggles of nations, of groups and individuals, for more freedom, emancipation, the abolition of illegitimate power-structures in the world? Has it any such task? How did it fulfil its task in the past? Did it betray this? What is the position today? The theme contains thousands of questions and those mentioned are certainly not all.

I

The first thing I want to say about this endless theme—and, however paradoxical it may sound, it amounts to a contribution of the Church to the freedom of the individual—is that Christian teaching as upheld by the Church holds, not that man is simply free but that real, true, total and definitive freedom consists in the eschatological possession of salvation itself which, although secretly effective in history, is the sheer gift of God bringing history to its end.

The normal adult human being has of course up to a point a psychological freedom of choice which in the last resort is not merely oriented to particular objects in his life but is identified with himself as one and whole and—through the transcendentality of this freedom of decision—places him beyond the particular deed and its individual objects in a free relationship to the ground of all reality and freedom, to God. However obscure in many respects the enigmas connected with this psychological freedom of choice may be, Christianity (at least Catholic Christianity) maintains firmly that it is the precondition of the salvation-event and of

[1] Cf. also Karl Rahner, *Toleranz in der Kirche* (Freiburg 1977).

man's final destiny: that is, it invites the individual always to allow for the fact that in the concrete course of his life he performs acts for which he can never entirely escape responsibility, even though reflection does not show him with absolute certainty what in his individual action is the result of his free decision and what is the result of the influence on him of already existing predetermining factors. But this freedom of choice— which can be realized at least by accepting or by protesting against the plain facts of his existence—does not itself simply make man free in the sense and in every respect in which he wants ultimately to be free or in the way freedom is promised him as definitive possession of salvation.

Creaturely freedom always starts out from internal (psychological) and external (historical and sociological) existing facts, always operates with existing material from which no further selection is made, and in this sense is always finite, limited and self-alienated. Subjectively infinite freedom is always restricted by the material on which it has to work. The individual (by what is in the last resort an act of self-deception) can regard his freedom as so much in harmony with the existing internal and external facts that he acquires a kind of philistine self-satisfaction and simply does not notice the hiatus between the subjectively infinite claim of freedom and the opportunities actually offered by the available material. For Christian anthropology however the repression of this unresolved hiatus in the last resort is not a laudable act of sober and unpretentious realism but the sin of a truly commonplace person renouncing his freedom's supreme claim to be infinite (explicitly or by repressing it), because he does not find any fulfilment immediately in himself or in the palpable and usable opportunities among the persons and things surrounding him.

The forthright realism of Christianity assures us that our freedom is finite, that the restrictedness and stubborn facts of the psychological, historical and sociological material of our freedom can never be abolished in the course of history, not even as a result of the greatest psychological and sociological changes for the better in our state of freedom; as long as our earthly history endures, we are always faced with the unresolved contradiction between the claim of our freedom and its actual opportunities; in this sense we are not free, our freedom can be liberated only by the act of God giving himself. This hard basic statement of Christian anthropology has a *dual* significance.

It disenchants man, who is always in danger of succumbing to the divine intoxication of his freedom's infinite claim, of thinking that it needs only one or another of the practicable changes in his internal or sociological situation for him to be infinitely free. Christianity deprives man of his illusion that infinite freedom can be attained in the course of history itself, shows him that man's impiety and self-destructiveness in the truest and most immediate sense of these terms lead him to look for such Utopias; that, by the very fact of struggling, albeit legitimately, for greater scope for psychological and sociological freedom, man continually produces *new limitations* of his own or another's freedom; that no possible genetic, psychological or sociological manipulation can produce the absolutely free human being, since this very manipulation must inevitably start out from certain limited, existing facts and then in turn produce the actual conditions for the other person's freedom and which are rightly regarded by the latter as restrictions of his freedom.

This kind of disenchantment has a truly positive significance in man's struggle for more freedom, for greater scope for freedom for the individual, for more and better material to be placed at the disposal of the individual for his free self-realization. It cannot of course be denied that this disenchantment carries with it the danger and the temptation—realized often enough in the history of Christianity—of abandoning the struggle for greater freedom, since everything might be changed but not improved, since every struggle for greater freedom only leads again and again to new constraints and self-alienations. If this terrible danger to Christian teaching on the freedom which in history always remains finite and on the permanent hiatus between the infinite claim of the subject of freedom and the historically always merely finite opportunities for the realization of freedom must always be seen clearly and continually brought to mind afresh in face of the guilt of historical Christianity, then this sober realism will have at bottom a positive significance precisely for the struggle for greater freedom.

The person thus disenchanted is better protected against Utopias in the bad sense: that is, against those which are the result of an outrageous monomania and assert the impossible claim to construct concrete reality in the light of a single principle, thus ultimately having a destructive influence on man. This realistic outlook prevents us from simply sacrificing man today to man tomorrow, from seeing the present merely and monotonously as that which must be outdated as quickly as possible by a future. Such sobriety can prevent a person from 'enjoying' the good opportunities of the present time with what is really a bad conscience, too readily open to suggestion: a bad conscience, since the present opportunities of freedom, being finite, derive their legitimacy *solely* from the fact that they can be surpassed and thus lead into a greater future. This Christian realism in estimating the actual opportunities of freedom has a further significance.

When a person does not succumb to an absolute banality of *carpe diem* in face of the finite scope of his freedom, he will not endure the un-resolved hiatus between the absolute claim of freedom and its finite opportunities of realization within history unless he believes and hopes in what Christianity calls the eternal Kingdom of God: the realization of absolute freedom for the immediate 'possession' of God, which is approached throughout the course of history but actually attained only by the consummation and dissolution of history. But if someone does believe and hope, he is free here and now in a unique way in regard to the finite goods of freedom which are presented to him to possess and enjoy. Hoping for an absolute fulfilment, he can place himself at a distance from his finite present; he does not need to make this absolute. But, as a result of this very realism, he can approach more frankly and courageously even a *future* that is possible in this world; he can take the risk of giving up his experience and enjoyment of the present for the sake of a merely creatively surmised, almost utopian future more easily and unhesitatingly than if he were faced with the dilemma *either* of having to defend *unconditionally* a present that is finite *or* of simply failing in the end to seize on a future that is not attained or is again unmasked as nothing more than a different form of internal or external constraints and self-alienations. A hopeful faith in a consummation of freedom by God is also a risk, and indeed the supreme risk of which man is capable; but it is only this faith which frees man from the necessity of clinging to the illusion that the future which can be realized in this world will one day be the realm of absolute freedom.

Christian realism in face of the opportunities of freedom within his-tory, rightly understood, does not paralyse man, forcing him to a passive acceptance of the present, to sterile conservatism, but gives him as a human being and a Christian the right to take a risk without the assur-ance of certain success, since success *and* failure are embraced together by the one promise of a definitive liberation of freedom for its immeasur-able consummation. If Christianity and the Church thus proclaim realis-tically the impossibility of a consummation of freedom within history, this does not mean that they have set up any concrete programmes and directives as to how even in the present world man can always struggle afresh to gain more scope for freedom in his interior and exterior existence while his history continues—which is certainly his duty—but they have given to man's freedom an infinite promise; this they give even to someone who perishes as a victim in this struggle within history; in an evenly balanced dialectic between present and future they protect the person who is rightly hungry for the future from what might be merely self-destructive Utopias. None of this of course means removing or minimizing the torment of individual historical decisions, the conflicts between concrete projects of an internal and external future of individuals and sociological groups, the harsh necessity of these conflicts and antagonisms; but for the individual all this struggle and all the risk is for a future which is always finite and uncertain, threatened by failure, but nevertheless enveloped by an ultimately ineffable peace, a future possessed by the person who knows that fidelity to conscience and unselfish service to others lead in the end to a fall into God's blessed freedom, whether this fall appears in the world to be victory or defeat. The Church's gospel of Christian realism is and remains the primary service that Christianity performs for the freedom of the individual and society.

II

Since this primary service belongs purely and simply to the nature of the gospel and the Church, I think that the Church has always provided it for man up to a point and in a variety of ways, often enough anonymously. That is not to deny of course that in its ministry and its people the Church has failed frequently and terribly to fulfil this task of promoting the freedom of the individual. Only too often, naively or culpably, it has certainly been associated with the powerful, presented its message as opium of the people, glorified in a conservative spirit the existing state of affairs which was not good and where freedom was lacking, and issued warnings against projects for the future which could have brought and often—contrary to its wishes and prognoses—did bring greater freedom. It is certainly therefore also the task of the Church honestly to admit the guilt it has incurred and in a spirit of self-criticism to ask how it might now and in the future better serve the individual's intramundane and sociological freedom. If raised here and now the question would have to be broken down into many individual questions and separate answers given to each of these.

Conscious of the fact that we are making a very arbitrary selection, we shall attempt to provide two answers in particular. Without giving a more detailed or precise explanation, we start out from the assumption that the Catholic Church, despite the permanence of its ultimate nature and its ultimate sociological structure, is open in principle to very far-reaching changes in its concrete structures. In the light of this assumption, if the Church would cautiously and courageously carry out such structural changes, we think that these changes in its own structure could be useful for the freedom of the individual in his secular life and promote the individual's freedom in secular society.

The fact that people in the Church believe in the living Lord of all history and in what he has promised to be the blessed outcome of this history; that people in the Church hope against all the hopelessness which is repeatedly justified by history; that there is prayer in the Church; that the Church regards itself as responsible for the poor and oppressed, for those who have had a raw deal in history and for the dead; that it prevents history (as J. B. Metz puts it) from being merely a history of the victors and those who have got off lightly; that the Church always maintains a position in the world from which both the assured tradition and the enticing future can be realistically and critically questioned and which does not permit any tangible reality in history to pretend, either in theory or in practice, to be God: these and many other things in the Church's faith and life can also be of the greatest importance for secular society in the future as they were in the past, more important than *we here* can explain. But, since we are asking about the importance of *structural change* in the Church for secular society and for the freedom of the individual and not about the importance of the Church as such for the world, the limitation imposed on our reflections here is legitimate and necessary.

Two possible consequences of structural change in the Church will now be considered. They can only be very vaguely indicated. And the question largely remains obscure and uncertain whether the peculiarities of this structural change in the Church *can* really have consequences for secular society: that is, whether and how such changes can be transferred into the secular sphere and can instigate analogous structures in secular society. If something of this kind were possible, if these new structures— which as such should be produced in the Church in the light of the latter's minority status—could be reproduced analogously in secular society, if the minority status of the Church were to force it—in view of its own needs—to form such structures *more rapidly* than is possible in secular society, then, despite the Church's minority status in a pluralist society, there might perhaps again come a time when the Church would not be trying to catch up with secular historical change but would be setting an example by going ahead of this. We certainly do not need to make our Christian faith and our membership of the Church dependent on *such* a hope, but neither should we *a priori* forbid this hope, as if it was certain that the Church's power to make history to a considerable extent in the present world had been clearly exhausted.

COMMON CONVICTIONS IN CHURCH AND SOCIETY

In order to come to the *primary* contribution of the Church envisaged here, we may start at a point which at first sight seems to have little to do with our problem. I venture to suggest that a secular society together with its institutions, even though it regards itself as liberal and pluralistic, cannot manage or exist without a certain foundation of common convictions respected by all who belong to that society. I do not think that this basis of common convictions—which cannot either consist in the very obvious usefulness of certain rules of life and institutionalisms or be replaced by the sheer brute force of the state—can simply consist in an absolutely inexhaustible heritage of tradition from the past or be continually regenerated simply and solely from man's nature, without society *itself* having the task, duty and necessity of deliberately working with its *own* means on the maintenance, necessary regeneration and transformation of this foundation. In the light of the dignity of every human being, I am also sure that in principle *all* have the power and opportunity to undertake the task of preserving and bringing this foundation up to date, but in the concrete it must be undertaken mainly by those who actually exercise power—that is, by the state. At the same time I assume that state and society are never identical in the concrete and that such an identity would not even be desirable. Desirable though it may be to break down power-structures, to eliminate the constraints and self-alienation in which human beings are involved, I also assume— because of the impossibility of considering adequately all processes of decision in the individual and in society and the consequent impossibility for authority (as determining cause of the individual's scope for freedom prior to his consent) to give *adequately* clear expression in institutional form to these processes of decision—that there will always be some who are more powerful and others less powerful in the state and therefore the task of preserving this foundation will lie with those who exercise power in a state and must be achieved by power.

In my opinion therefore the only question can be *how* the power of the state attempts concretely to obtain the necessary and continually freshly renewed regeneration of the foundation of common convictions and rules of life necessary to a society, while leaving as much scope as possible for freedom of opinion and freedom to shape one's own life. As can be seen at a glance anywhere in the world, without going into details here, this continually renewed attempt to establish the coexistence of freedom of opinion together with its public manifestation and concrete realization on the one hand and of the positive cultivation on the other of a common sociological basic conviction in the whole world, in communist and western (democratic or more or less authoritarian) societies and states, is a very difficult task and cannot be solved simply by a radical option for one side or the other. And, if we take seriously the historicity of all human truth, it is also obvious that it is impossible to find any formal principles which could simply be applied in order to solve the problem once and for all in a concrete society and to spare the latter the embarrassment of seeking, experimenting and struggling for an historical decision without a visible arbitrator. On the other hand, this does not mean that it is impossible to develop better models than those which previously existed to show how this continually renewed struggle between freedom of opinion and the necessity of a common 'ideology' of society (if the term is understood in a neutral sense) can be conducted with mutual respect and a balance—even though precarious and always merely temporary—be found between the two coexisting factors. It can be stated here without further arguments that such new models are necessary but largely lacking in secular society everywhere in the world.

In this respect the Church with its structures and structural changes might set an example but is not yet in a position to do so adequately, since it has not yet properly developed the models for the balance of authority and freedom in the internal life of the Church which its minority status requires it to provide. In the past the Church undoubtedly developed for the protection of its common beliefs authoritarian forms which are no longer effective today in view of its minority status and the impossibility of appealing to the 'secular arm', when the person against whose opinion the protest of the Church and its magisterium is directed accepts in principle the Church's teaching authority. Even for authentic declarations of the magisterium a comparatively wide consensus in the Church's sense of faith and in the Church's theology is an assumption without which the magisterium cannot act legitimately at all and still less be really effective. With the present pluralism in theology, which can never be completely overcome, with the frequent absence of obviously common horizons of understanding, with historical or historicist reflection on the formerly wholly disregarded horizons of understanding, assumptions and their historical relativity, a statement of the Church's magisterium commonly recognized as binding on all and understood by all is no longer so easy. A statement of this kind, which the Church's magisterium finds it easy to make in an authentic but not defining declaration, will mostly not be very effectively binding or make a very effective impact on the actual awareness of the Church's members.

New definitions of the magisterium today however, as distinct from those of former times in a different mental climate and in a different climate of belief, presuppose so many conditions that are difficult to fulfil that definitions going beyond an emphatic repetition of older defined statements can be expected only rarely or not at all in the future. The historically considered or unconsidered variety of horizons of understanding which cannot be really synthesized in the concrete awareness of the individual or of the officials of the Church's magisterium, over and above the difficulties which have always existed, today create an increasingly disturbing question as to whether even the officially valid formulations of faith really express the same beliefs as those which are present in the awareness of the individual members of the Church and of the diverse groups in the Church. The doctrine of the hierarchy of truths in the Second Vatican Council and the ecumenical efforts to bring about a union of the Churches which will not involve the abandonment of diversity in their histories of faith also show that the uniformity of the sense of faith as conceived in the measures of the Church's magisterium in the past as its presupposition and task is not so easy to maintain and establish as it was once thought. In addition there are all the peculiarities of the human condition today for which the Church's magisterium must make allowances in a way different from that adopted in former times when the good faith of the individual believer or theologian apparently deviating from the Church's sense of faith was not taken for granted as it must be today in a society that proclaims freedom of conscience.

With what has just been said and much more that really ought to be added, we do not mean of course that we in the Church know already *how today* as distinct from formerly the authority of the ecclesial community of the same faith and the authority of freedom must be made mutually compatible, what institutionalisms there ought to be in the Church today so that authority and the enduring importance of the magisterium can coexist in a positive (even though perhaps always somewhat strained) fashion with freedom of conscience, the further historical *development* of the Church's sense of faith—which cannot simply be controlled by the teaching office—with the legitimate freedom of theology and with the diversity of the development of the individual's sense of faith, which is not simply identical with the Church's sense of faith and which may nevertheless be publicly made known. Nor of course does what we have said mean that *secular* society must adopt the same style as that in which the *Church* in the future must overcome the difficulties involved in our question. For this, sociological and ecclesial awareness are too diverse in origin, content and goal. But, since the new problems arising here for the Church *and* for secular society to a large extent have a common cause, by working more quickly on this question and finding more quickly forms of institution to cope with the outstanding problems, the Church could also set an example for secular society as long as it did not relapse into a more or less medieval set-up but were to look for a way in which freedom of thought *and* the maintenance and further development of a common basic conviction, without which a society must break down, can coexist and exercise a vital influence on one another.

I shall not attempt to put forward any further considerations as to how in the Church a liberal, anti-authoritarian and yet effective function of the Church's magisterium could be conceived today or tomorrow. For this a long haul would be required; and, incidentally, it must also be remembered that the politically constituted secular society on the one hand and the Church within a pluralistic society on the other are distinguished by the fact that it is not possible to get out of the former while it is possible to leave the latter, resulting in a very complicated dialectic of a dual character with reference to strictness and mildness in interpreting the different requirements for membership of the one or the other society. For this question also a new ecclesiology needs to be developed with reference to an ecclesiological marginality—a state which is still mainly considered as that of the 'catechumen', which does not get us much further.

A theology of the coexistence of apparently merely logically inconsistent propositions ought to be developed, so far as these exist on existentially and sociologically different planes and in this light are by no means actually 'incompatible'. So we might continue. But it is not possible now. All that can be said is that the Church ought to develop new ways of acting and new forms of institution for the coexistence in the Church of freedom of belief and a commonly binding profession of faith; since such a development can be more rapid (if we want it to be), the Church could set an example up to a point for the solution of an analogous problem of modern society, which is more or less helpless in face of the dilemma between an ideology of society and the state imposed by authority and an increasingly rapid disappearance of common basic convictions without which society cannot exist except by being turned into anarchy or being placed under the tyranny of an enforced ideology.

THE CHURCH AS MINORITY IN SOCIETY

In a minority situation in which neither the Church itself nor its ministry is supported by the power of the secular society, it is clear that the groups freely emerging at the base must and will acquire quite a new importance for the Church as such and also for its ministry and for the effectiveness of the latter. Of course we ought now to explain more precisely what this means, how initiatives for such free activity from the base were developed at Vatican II, what trends exist for a further development of these initiatives, how greatly such efforts have been frustrated since the council, whether and under what conditions and assumptions these more personal basic communities can be regarded as basic cells of the Church today, how they are related to traditional parishes, what new image of the priest and his function can and must be derived from them. And so on. We cannot go into all these things here. But, in this minority situation in which the Church is no longer propped up by secular sociological powers, it is obvious that it can be seen increasingly only as a Church from below and no longer (from the sociological standpoint) as a Church *facing* its people, that relations between base and ministry will and must be given a form very different from that to which we have been accustomed. Similarly structures and institutions must be changed.

It seems to me however that an analogous problem exists in secular society. Whether it is a question of western democracies with their very diverse interpretations of the term 'democracy' or of socialist countries with their very diverse forms of party-oligarchies, everywhere in the world the relationship between the mass, the base, the people, on the one hand, and the élitist controlling bodies on the other seems to be disturbed. The distance between the two sides seems to be too great; parliamentary representative democracy is losing respect and not infrequently gives the impression that it is merely a *façade* behind which other forces and agencies exercise uncontrolled power, the *identity* of these small and mostly anonymous groups holding power being *in the last resort* irrelevant. And if in socialist countries the people is supposed to be the active carrier of the economy and the state itself, here too—as a result of the various attempts to find really genuinely practicable models—it can be seen that the basic *problem* remains the same: *how*—that is, on what principles and with what technical means—the enormous mass of a people, educated up to a point and consequently not to be kept in a state of tutelage, can be brought into closer contact with the indispensable machinery of the higher functionaries so that a decision by the people itself becomes possible. In this matter also situation, task and means are quite certainly very different in the Church and in secular society. But the active participation from below on the part of the base in the decisions of the controlling powers represents a problem common to Church and society. There is a search for new forms and structures for this participation; even in the West we cannot assume that everything is clear in regard to this question and that we must merely be loyal to the democratic constitution or shape one in a purer form.

Might not the Church in its own sphere develop a model solution to this problem which could then be helpful to those trying to cope with the same problem in the secular sphere? Long ago it was said: 'See how these Christians love one another.' Could we hope that one day people might say: 'See how they really live *with* one another in *freedom* and with as few constraints as possible'? All this is of course very vague and the hope just expressed is consequently very utopian, particularly since there is still scarcely any understanding or desire in the Church for such far-reaching structural changes and since such an attitude will presumably become more obvious and inescapable only when the Church and its ministry are made more generally aware of the minority status of the Church and its inexorable consequences. But might not the Church's sense of responsibility for secular society, proclaimed afresh at Vatican II, permit it to become more clearly aware of its duty and more determined so to shape its own structures for the relationship between base and ministry that they will provide a valuable example also for secular society and for the realization of the freedom of the individual; that the old models will not continue to be the basis of human life together in the Church long after they have been abandoned as obsolete in secular society?

5

THEOLOGICAL JUSTIFICATION OF THE CHURCH'S DEVELOPMENT WORK

ON THE theme here presented for our reflections, as it is expressed in the title, from the very nature of the case, more could and really should be said and said more precisely than is possible in these few pages. With the reservation, then, that much that is important and perhaps more fundamental is being disregarded, we may put forward here some reflections on the question why even apparently secular development aid is one of the tasks which the Church by its very nature must undertake, although of course development aid is never a task and obligation for the Church (for its authority and its people) alone. But at this very point the question arises: why must the Church *also* be concerned with development aid if other sociological agencies and authorities are mainly bound to do the same thing? The question becomes even more difficult when we recall the fact that the Church can have and will have an ultimate—its own specific—motivation for such a task, but evidently may not regard the latter merely as a means to an end (openly or tacitly), as a means to those tasks and ends at which it aims by its very nature: that is, it must not see and utilize development aid as publicity material and as a way of entry for the evangelization and Christianization of the peoples, as a superficial reading, for instance, of the Decree of Vatican II on missionary activity might suggest.[1] In its radical form therefore the question is obviously: How can a task be that of the Church as such and at the same time remain within what seems to be essentially a wholly secular sphere?

Although it seems to hold also for other activities which the Church

---

[1] Second Vatican Council, *Ad Gentes* 11–12.

still undertakes today, this idea seems to contradict *a priori* that distinction, which has become increasingly clear in recent centuries and has been increasingly accepted unreservedly by the Church, between the religious sphere properly so called, for which the Church is responsible, and the secular sphere, for which secular society has a more or less independent responsibility. In raising this question we assume that development aid is really a genuine task for the Church and not merely undertaken in a subsidiary fashion when those who are properly called to the work do not sufficiently match up to their task and responsibility. In answering this question we assume moreover that a task which is that of churchgoing Christians is also that of the Church as such (to some extent and in some way), even though this assumption leaves many questions still open and many distinctions disregarded which should be considered if we regard the task of Christians as that of the Church. Despite the many problems it involves, this assumption can presumably be made here, since *Misereor** —of its nature and despite its more or less official ecclesiastical character—is based, at least for its effectiveness, on the free will of individual Christians in the Church.

We shall try to answer the question from two aspects: that of love and that of hope, since the Church must be a community of love and the eschatological hope of the world.

Has there been sufficient and sufficiently radical reflection in the Church's traditional theology[2] on the words of Jesus making Christian existence and salvation consist in a duality—not in itself bad—of love of God and love of neighbour which can be raised up to a higher unity, a duality in which, as a unity, the two commandments are equal to one another? Has this theology been sufficiently influenced and challenged to radical reflection by Paul's saying that whoever loves his neighbour has fulfilled the law? Has the theology of the unity of love of God and love of neighbour, which is put forward in a rudimentary form in in the first letter of John, really become a theme which is squarely faced in traditional theology? Has there been sufficient reflection on the fact that, accord-

---

* The fund-raising organization for overseas aid set up by the German Catholic bishops. It is wholly concerned with material help and has nothing to do with missionary activity.— Translator.

[2] On what follows see Karl Rahner, 'Über die Einheit von Gottes- und Nächstenliebe', in *Schriften zur Theologie,* vol. VI (Zurich 1965), pp. 277–98; ET 'Reflections on the Unity of the Love of Neighbour and the Love of God,' in *Theological Investigations,* vol. VI (Baltimore/London 1969), pp. 231–49.

ing to Jesus' speech on the judgement in Matthew 25, men are judged—it might almost be said 'atheistically'—solely in the light of their attitude to their neighbour?

Imagine that these (and similar) texts, to which we have just referred, were not in sacred Scripture but had been formulated by a modern theologian. What would 'normal' theology then say? It would certainly say that love of neighbour is indeed a commandment of the infinite, holy God, the observance of which is binding on anyone who wants to love God with his whole heart and must therefore fulfil his commandments; the two precepts however cannot be placed alongside one another as of equal importance, but the second must be subsumed under the first as a simple and somewhat remote conclusion from it. This theology would say that love of neighbour is far from being the fulfilment of the whole law. It would say that it is possible to know for certain by reason and faith the existence of a personal God, although we cannot see him, and hence we can have a personal relationship with him that is not brought about by loving our neighbour whom we do see, even though this love of neighbour is a commandment of the same God and must be fulfilled. This theology would say that it is an unpardonable curtailment of the idea of the last judgement to suggest that man is not judged there according to the first tablet of the Law.

Of course it cannot be our task here to give an adequate answer exegetically, systematically and existentially-ontologically to the problems indicated. But evidently such an answer must bring out a greater unity and a clearer mutual integration of love of God and love of neighbour than is suggested in the theory of run-of-the-mill theology as outlined above. Love of neighbour (we are only indicating a possible way towards a solution), when it reaches its full nature and its ultimate depths, must itself be explicitly or perhaps only unthematically and implicitly but nevertheless truly love of God; real love of God, which enables us to love and is productive of salvation, cannot be attained in a purely theoretical reflection (however important this may be), but only at the point where and when a person achieves that total self-realization and that radical self-transcendence which in fact is brought about only in love for our neighbour and there knows, at least unthematically, what is meant by God as condition of the possibility of such personal self-transcendence. If what we have just suggested is correct (as the presupposition of a full understanding of the words of Scripture to which we referred and whose importance must not be minimized), then we must conclude that in the last resort (despite the distinction between love of God and love of neighbour and despite a categorial pluralism of the concrete realizations of love of neighbour in individual cases and in the different requirements of life and society) love of neighbour is not an individual task to be fulfilled within a particular *area* of human life, but a universal determinant of human existence as one and whole, a determinant which must expressly or tacitly affect and make its mark on all that is good and salvational in human life.

In the whole extent of categorial, historical and sociological life there are of course many realities and achievements which are different, do not mean the same, among which one can be present while the other is absent. But, as distinct from individual tasks and achievements in this historical and sociological spatiotemporality, that which really can and must be called love of neighbour in its basic nature is more deeply rooted in human existence and thus brings the totality of this existence and not merely one area of it to its true and full nature and in fact to God. From this standpoint (if what has been said were developed at greater length and more precisely substantiated) it could be made clear that in principle in human life there must always be a thematicized, explicitly religious attitude and worship of God, but that this does not mean that love of neighbour is merely a particular area of this human life, lying outside the field of man's relationship to God and thus linked with that relationship at most by a formally conceived precept of this God. When it reaches its real and full nature and is really selfless (not merely a reasonable compromise between egoisms), love of neighbour is itself a religious attitude, love of God, whether it explicitly thematizes this nature of its own or not.

From all this we may conclude on the other hand that explicitly denominational religion expressed in specific forms of worship (in the purity and radicalness in which it comes to us from revelation and grace) cannot be indifferent to its own self-realization precisely in love of neighbour, discovers itself in its full nature only if it abandons itself and loses itself up to a point to those dimensions of an apparently secular, worldly character in which the 'secular' and 'worldly' realizations of love of neighbour take place. To some extent love of God must forget itself in love of neighbour in order to reach its own full nature and simultaneously its ever freshly productive source. What at first sight is the secularity of love of neighbour is the source and sphere of realization of the love of God itself as such. The secular world exists where it is the sphere of man's total self-realization (which it can and ultimately must be, since love of neighbour must be concretely realized in the 'world'), established as such by love of neighbour—which is love of God—since the latter needs this space in which love really seeks and finds the other person, without returning to itself or being absorbed in itself.

At this point two things must be remembered. Firstly, the Church as one and not merely as the external sum-total of individuals, and also as an historical and sociological factor, is the subject of love of God and neighbour. As one it must realize and attest love of neighbour in historical and sociological tangibility. It must do so always out of love of God, but truly out of self-forgetting love of neighbour, reaching and remaining with the other person and precisely in this way finding its own ground and its own potential, which is love of God: thus love of God and love of neighbour justify one another mutually in their distinction and unity. The secularity, the very worldliness of the world is consequently the field also of the self-realization of the Church as one, in so far as the latter is the sociologically constituted community of love. Secondly, love of neighbour—at least today in the present state of the world in which sociological structures are not merely simple facts, but also the object of man's freedom to plan—is not merely a private relationship between individuals within the static, existing structures of society. Love of neighbour has as its concrete object the changing of these sociological conditions under which love of neighbour as a private activity has to be practised. Changing society in order to provide more opportunities of love of neighbour, man's sociopolitical and socio-critical task, the struggle for greater freedom and justice: all these are requirements and tasks of love of neighbour, if the latter is understood rightly, in this rapidly changing but planned society. And thus—at least today—the love which the Church is expected to live and attest by its action has also this task. It shares the task, as we said at the very beginning, with other sociological groups and authorities, even though its relationship in the task with these other groups and authorities cannot be more precisely defined. But it cannot simply leave this task merely to other groups and authorities alone, since it would otherwise betray the love of neighbour which in fact it must itself practise and attest and which it cannot simply leave to others.

Misereor must be seen against this background of understanding (here of course merely indicated and needing more profound and precise expression in a variety of ways). At the same time—important as this question is in itself—we are not concerned here with the constitution and the exact legal status of *Misereor*. Whether *Misereor* (although inaugurated and promoted by authority from above) is to be seen more as an institution formed and sustained from the base of the Church or as a really official ecclesiastical agency or as a mixture of the two possibilities, of which there are many examples in the Church, need not be considered here. For both authority and the people of the Church (also as such) are charged with the task of active love: a love that goes out to the other person in the 'world' and is not understood as a means to something else, however sublime; a love that carries with it a will to justice and, today at least, has also sociopolitical tasks; a love that carries with it as its condition and ultimate ground God's love for us as it became eschatologically irreversible and victorious in Jesus Christ and our love for God in Jesus Christ. But this is a love that can become so 'worldly' precisely because it has to be given to our neighbour purely and simply, and not only to those who belong to the household of the faith, because it must be extended as widely as God's love for man is itself extended. In a word, it is love seen from the Christian standpoint: not merely an inward disposition, but something that must be realized in action in which alone a person really gets away from himself. The peculiarity of *Misereor* is that it is a task—and one which is particularly urgent in the present world-situation—of that love which constitutes the Church and which in the last resort is the only total and comprehensive way of access to the knowledge of God and to his love.

We must consider *Misereor* from yet another aspect, in order to make clear up to a point at least its theological location. In the Dogmatic Constitution, *Lumen Gentium*, of Vatican II, in n35, we read that lay-people ought to show themselves to be 'children of the promise, . . . strong in faith and *hope*', awaiting the glory to come. This hope (says the Council) they must not conceal in the depths of their hearts, but must express it in turning to God and in struggle 'even in the framework of secular life'. Christian hope of definitive freedom, reconciliation and glory, being an eschatological gift of God and not the autonomous work of man realizable in history, is often under suspicion as 'opium of the people', as destructive of the courage and action needed in the historical struggle in the present world for greater freedom and justice. There should really be no dispute about the fact that in practice Christian eschatological hope has often exercised an influence in this wrong direction. In this connection it would be possible to produce plenty of factual evidence and even passages from the declarations of the magisterium. But in principle this is not and cannot be the situation, even though the ultimate proof of the opposite cannot be established by theoretical considerations or by referring back to the past history of the Church with its contributions to greater freedom and justice and emancipation, but only by the action of Christians *today* for a better world and its society. In principle it must be clear that the eschatological hope of Christians for a final reconciliation does not discourage or weaken the struggle for a better world here and now, but even endows that struggle with a final absoluteness, despite the relativity and provisional character of all that it can achieve in the course of history.

The eschatological hope of Christians awaits the consummation dissolving history as sovereign deed and gift of God himself, since this consummation in God's self-communication (called grace and glory) consists in an immediacy which alone can reconcile and dissolve the contradictions of this world. But this eschatological gift of God is addressed to man's act of freedom and can reach the latter only by producing this very act by its own power. This act of freedom, which accepts the gift of God, is realized however, not only in a dimension of interiority, of spirituality, of mysticism, of a quietist and pietist attitude, but in all the breadth and depth of human existence which (as indicated above) is essentially also love of neighbour. The other person, who is loved, is the sacrament in which we receive God. But this also means essentially that Christian hope is brought to its own nature and its own fullness by an *intra*mundane hope. If this were not so, how could the Council say that the eschatological hope of Christians must also find expression 'in the framework of secular life', through the *vitae saecularis structurae*? If God's eternal life is to be hoped for in truth and action, this cannot come about by making absolute in practice the goods of this world as they exist in the concrete, while getting a kind of reassurance from the fact that eternal life is granted at the moment when the goods of this world and this life, once held absolutely firmly, are snatched away from us.

Christian hope can be what it must be as a genuine and total act of life only if it relativizes the goods we possess and is *thus* in truth and not merely in an optimal pious ideology a profession of faith in God's eternal life. This relativization however is not merely negative. It makes us free for other possibilities in the present world. It relativizes the here and now existing (sometimes positive) realities of life and society; it makes us free and open for future possibilities of history and society; it makes us free for an unprejudiced approach to a still open, uncontrollable and even dangerous future; it is a critique and rejection of a false, merely static conservatism, defending only things as they exist, without courage for risk or for any experiment which cannot be adequately calculated at every turn. Anyone who really has a genuine eschatological hope and wants to realize it can do so only by acquiring a real receptivity for an open future in the present world. The Christian should really be the last person to cling absolutely to what remains of his present happiness, while explaining merely ideologically that in his pietist interiority he also has his mind on eternity. In order to hope for what is not yet possessed, it is necessary also to let go of what we possess here and now. This holds for the Christian in his hope also for the sociological dimensions in which his love and his hope must (also) be realized and brought home to themselves. Only someone who is prepared here for change and experiment—which, despite all necessary planning, can never be adequately calculated in advance—can be a hoping Christian, whose hope also decides his eternal salvation. In his hope the Christian rises above all attempts to establish autonomously as a secular Utopia the definitive kingdom of reconciliation and above a hardened conservatism clinging absolutely to present possessions, since he does not know (beyond what can clearly be calculated) whether something better is coming in the future.

Misereor then is an action and institution of Christian hope. *Misereor* demands aid which makes the helper poorer without promising him that in the long term (which he perhaps will not experience himself) his assistance will turn out to be clearly and certainly advantageous and useful to him. In the last resort *Misereor* does not appeal to a well-understood self-interest, but to the hope of eternal life which implies courage and power to give up intramundane values already possessed in an act of faith which by this very fact realizes and simultaneously attests hope in God himself. Development aid, regarded as a purely secular effort to provide economic assistance, might be no more than a desperate attempt to balance off a number of egoisms (perhaps justified in themselves) against each other. To this secular enterprise *Misereor* brings a surplus of courage for unselfish, self-risking adventure, without denying that the same kind of loving hope might also exist outside the Church as a sociological institution, among 'anonymous' Christians.

We have attempted to make clear the fact that, in the present-day unity of the world and in its sociological and economic situation, development aid is required as task and duty also and particularly from the Church if the latter is really to be seen as the community of Christian love and hope. If it has such a task, then its activity enters into the secular field of the world. This must not be merely the disposition and action of individual Christians, but also the action of the Church as such, whether represented by its authority or by groups which expressly belong to it. We have thus touched on the problem why and how—despite the actual autonomy of the world with its own spheres of action—the Church as such can and must make its impact on this field and be made relevant within this dimension, without setting out the implications of the problem and still less producing a solution of it. But it seems that the theological problem *qua* theological must not necessarily be considered here. For if we do not adopt a totalitarian theory of the state, assigning to the latter alone all sociopolitical questions and tasks, but concede to other sociological groups their autonomous right to undertake such tasks in a free pluralist and democratic society, then we cannot deny the same right to the Church also in our society when it claims this in the light of its own self-understanding.

PART FOUR

Future of the Church

6

BASIC THEOLOGICAL INTERPRETATION
OF THE SECOND VATICAN COUNCIL

I F WE are to discuss here a basic theological interpretation of the Second Vatican Council, it is certainly appropriate to make a few preliminary remarks about the treatment of the essential theme. If we speak of a basic interpretation, we mean one which is not imposed on the Council from outside, but suggested by the Council itself, so that here basic nature and basic interpretation amount to the same thing. The assumption of this basic interpretation is of course the fact and the assurance that this Council, despite the historical contingencies involved in such an event, was not merely an arbitrary accumulation of individual events and decisions, but an internal essential coherence of incidents which was not produced merely by its formal juridical character. At the same time and in the last resort it is irrelevant how far, how clearly and how urgently the organizers of the Council had this basic conception explicitly in mind. If the meaning and nature of existentially important events in the life of an individual human being encompass more than this individual explicitly objectifies and aims at in his consciousness, this is even more true of important events in the history of the Church which to a specifically unique extent are under the direction of the Spirit of the Church. If we are able to say about John XXIII's explicit intentions in regard to the Council not much more than that this Pope regarded a council as appropriate and opportune even after Vatican I with its 'papalism' and that he wanted a 'pastoral' council, this does not mean that a basic theological conception of a deeper and more comprehensive kind was not possible.

We are looking for a basic *theological* interpretation, because—without being able here to enter more precisely into the problem of the relationship between theology and church history—we think that church history is specifically distinct from secular history and in the last resort has to describe particularly the *history of the nature* of the Church, a nature which both supplies the hermeneutic principle of church history and is itself—as nature in history—revealed from this history in a mutual relationship of dependence.

Difficult as it may be to understand and although it can be expressed only in a rudimentary way, we must attempt to formulate in advance the basic idea with which the question raised is concerned, so that we do not lose sight of the coherence of the many individual observations and individual considerations. What we are saying is that the Second Vatican Council is the beginning of a tentative approach by the Church to the discovery and official realization of itself as *world-Church*. This thesis may seem exaggerated and it certainly needs to be explained much more precisely before it can be made to sound acceptable. It is of course also misleading if only because the Church was always *in potentia* world-Church and because the actualizing of this potentiality itself involved a long historical process of coming-to-be, the origins of which coincide with the beginning of European colonialism and of the modern world-mission of the Church from the sixteenth century, an actualizing which is not completely finished even today. But if we look at the macroscopic and official action of the Church and at the same time become more clearly aware that the concrete, real activity of the Church—despite the contradiction to its own nature involved in its attitude to the world outside Europe—was what we might venture to describe as that of an export firm, exporting to the whole world a European religion along with other elements of this supposedly superior culture and civilization, and not really attempting to change the commodity, then it seems appropriate and justified to regard Vatican II as the first great official event in which the Church came to be realized *as world*-Church.

There were of course precedents for this event: for example, the consecration of native bishops (but for the most part only in the present century), the discontinuance in missionary practice of Europeanisms which had been consolidated by Rome in the Eastern Rites controversy, and so on. The significance of these precedents is not to be concealed or minimized, but it must also be observed that they had no repercussions on the European–North American church until their influence began to be felt at Vatican II. At that point they could be seen simply as precedents for what we observed—albeit only rudimentarily and tentatively, often overlaid by the former style of the European church—at Vatican II, when a world-Church began to act as such with all its parts exercising a reciprocal influence on one another.

In this general thesis on the basic conception of Vatican II, as already mentioned, it cannot be denied that the actualization of the Church's nature as world-Church was manifested at the Council only in a very rudimentary way and hesitatingly. Nor can it be concealed that there are movements in the opposite direction. Can we be certain, for instance, that the danger will be avoided in the coming years of the new canon law, now being prepared in Rome, emerging as a western canon law but being imposed on the world-Church in Latin America, Asia and Africa? Have not the Roman Congregations always had the mentality of a centralized bureaucracy, claiming to know what is best everywhere in the world for the service of the Kingdom of God and the salvation of souls and do not their decisions appear to be shockingly naive, based as they are on the assumption that the Roman or Italian mentality is the obvious standard of judgement? It must of course be admitted that the theoretical problems arising from the Europeanization of the Church are anything but clear. Must the marital morality of the Masai in East Africa be substantially no more than a repetition of the morality of European Christianity or would it not be possible for an African chief, even if he is a Christian, to live in the style of the Patriarch Abraham? Must the Eucharist be celebrated even in Alaska with wine from the grape? These and similar questions perhaps not infrequently present theoretical impediments to the actualization of the world-Church as such. Together with many other reasons they explain why the great official actualization of the world-Church as such was manifested only more or less rudimentarily and hesitantly at Vatican II. At the Mass before the individual sessions, in which the different rites of the Church were represented, there was still no African dancing to be seen.

Finally, in regard to the manifestation of the world-Church as such at the Council and afterwards, the fact cannot be overlooked that the individual cultures in the world, to which the Church must be culturally adapted in order to be a world-Church, are themselves involved today in change to an extent and at a speed hitherto unknown, so that it is not easy to say what really valuable material for the future the individual cultures might offer to enable this Church really to become a world-Church. Whatever may be the answer to this question, it cannot be denied that the Church was officially manifested at the highest level at

Vatican II for the first time *as world*-Church. In what follows this statement will be more concretely substantiated, considered and questioned in regard to future consequences.

In the first place the Council was for the first time in a formal way a Council of the world-Church as such. We need only compare it with Vatican I to see its uniqueness in the formal juridical sense. It is true that there were representatives of episcopal sees in Asia or Africa present at Vatican I. But these were missionary bishops of European or American origin. At that time there was not yet a native episcopate anywhere in the Church. But one appeared at Vatican II. Perhaps this was far from being proportionate to the representation from European episcopates. But it was there. These bishops did not come as individual, simple visitors, *ad limina* to give an account of their dioceses and to take home missionary alms; Vatican II really was a first assembly of the world-episcopate, not acting as an advisory body to the Pope, but with him and under him as itself the supreme teaching and decision-making authority in the Church. There really was a world-council with a world-episcopate such as had not hitherto existed and with its own autonomous function. The actual significance of the non-European part of this total episcopate may have been comparatively slight; the consequences of this conciliar event for the post-conciliar life of the Church may still be very limited, as the Roman synods of bishops have shown since then; none of this alters the essential fact that the Council made manifest and brought into activity a Church which was no longer the European church with its American areas of dissemination and its exports to Asia and Africa. Here, under the guise of a natural and gradual development, something like a qualitative leap took place, even though this new nature of a world-Church that is not only *in potentia* but also *in actu* is still largely obscured by the particular characteristics of the older European church.

The meaning of this leap to the world-Church can be seen more clearly in a glance at the decrees of this council. The Constitution on the Liturgy—as far as the use of the vernacular is concerned—may already be essentially obsolete; without it and without the Council the victory of the vernacular would not have been conceivable. Latin had its origins in secular life and there became the common standard language of educated people. It was *for this reason* and not really for any other that it became the language of the liturgy in the western Church and remained so long after it had lost its importance elsewhere. But, as the language of a small and particular cultural sphere, Latin could not be the language of a world-Church. The victory of the vernacular languages in the Church's liturgy is a clear and urgent signal of the coming-to-be of a world-Church, with its particular churches each existing autarchically in its own cultural group, rooted in that culture and no longer exported from Europe. It is of course also the signal of all the new problems of a world-Church whose non-European particular churches—despite their bonds with Rome—can no longer be governed by Europe and the European mentality.

In *Gaudium et Spes,* in an act of the whole Church as such, the Church as a whole became expressly aware of its responsibility for the future history of mankind. Although in detail it is largely the expression of a European mentality, the fact remains that this Constitution reveals the presence of the Third World as part of the Church and as the object of the latter's responsibility. Although it is only with great difficulty and terribly slowly that European churchgoers are becoming aware of the Church's world-responsibility, this responsibility, political theology, can no longer be excluded from the consciousness of a world-Church.

As far as the dogmatic decrees of the Council—on the Church and on Divine Revelation—are concerned, much that is said there emerges from a specifically European mentality and the problems considered are mainly or solely relevant to a European theology. But it can be said that an effort has been made in these decrees to produce statements that are not much affected by the linguistic style of a neoscholastic theology and can be more easily made intelligible in the whole world. This becomes more obvious if we compare these texts with the corresponding late neoscholastic schemata which had been prepared in Rome before the Council. It is possible also to point to the fact that in the teaching on the episcopate as a whole and its function in the Church and on the importance of regional particular churches doctrinal assumptions were set up or elucidated which are fundamental to the Church's understanding of itself as world-Church. We may well think that the Constitution on revelation—which assumes that revelation begins in the Old Testament, with Abraham—does not exactly present a concept of 'revelation' which is easily accessible to African and Asian cultures, particularly since the millennia between 'primitive revelation' and Abraham remain unfilled.

We can however show that the Council in its teaching did two things which are of fundamental importance for a world-wide missionary activity. In the Declaration on the Relationship of the Church to Non-Christian Religions, for the first time in the history of the Church's teaching, the way was prepared for a positive appraisal of the great world-religions. Moreover, in the Constitution on the Church, in the Decree on the Church's Missionary Activity and in *Gaudium et Spes,* a salvific will of God—even after the Fall—is proclaimed as so universal and effective that it can be restricted only by a person's decision made with a bad conscience and at no other point; an opportunity of really salvific faith in revelation is admitted even outside Christian verbal revelation, which is such that—by comparison with earlier theology—basic assumptions for the world-Church's world-mission are created which had not previously existed. It is against this background that we can see the Declaration on Religious Freedom, in which the Church expressly renounces for all situations in the whole world the use of any powers in proclaiming its message that are not implied in the power of the gospel itself. Everyone knows what a great impediment the division of the Churches in Christendom is to the propagation of Christianity in the whole world, in what were known as the 'missionary countries'. That is why all ecumenical activities which the Council itself developed, approved or instigated, must be appreciated as contributions of the Council to Christianity's becoming a world-Church. In a word, at this Council, at least in a rudimentary way, the Church in its teaching began to act *as* a world-Church. We might say that, under the still largely existing phenotype of a European and North American Church, it made itself apparent as the genotype of a world-Church as such.

Perhaps however we can attempt to grasp this process of the coming-to-be of a world-Church at a somewhat deeper level. Those who are concerned with ecclesiastical historiography rightly struggle continually to find a theologically appropriate division of church history. At least it is clear that the division of European history into antiquity, Middle Ages and modern times is not a theologically satisfying scheme for church history. We are of course leaving aside here the question of a theologically appropriate subdivision of the great epochs of church history. Moreover, in regard to history in general and the history of the Church in particular, we are sure that there is not as much happening nor is it equally important in each individual section of history, measured as a period of time, while a comparatively short period of time can represent a great epoch in history. In the light of these assumptions, from the theological standpoint, we can say that there are three great epochs in church history, the third of which has only just begun and was authoritatively brought to notice at Vatican II:

1. The short period of Judaeo-Christianity;
2. The period of the Church in a particular cultural group, that of Hellenism and European culture and civilization;
3. The period in which the Church's living space is from the very outset the whole world.

These three periods, representing three essential basic situations of Christianity, of its proclamation and of the Church, distinct from each other, can of course for their own part be subdivided in a very far-reaching way: so, for instance, the second period by the caesurae marking the transition from antiquity to the Middle Ages and the transition from medieval civilization at the time of European colonialism and of the Enlightenment; at the same time the causes of these caesurae—which are frequent and nevertheless connected with each other—would have to be made clear.

I think that this tripartite division of church history as such is theologically correct, even though the first period was very brief. This first period of Judaeo-Christianity (together with its own specific repercussions through Jewish proselytism and the phenomenon of the 'God-fearers', the *eusebomenoi,* known from Philo, the Acts of the Apostles and Jewish propaganda literature) derives its peculiarity and singularity from the fact that its mental climate is that of the fundamental Christian salvation-event as such—the death and resurrection of Jesus himself—and the proclamation of this event *within* its *own* historical situation (not in any other situation) is in fact proclamation in Israel and to Israel. Precisely because something like a mission to the Gentiles had become completely conceivable on this basis, it is clear that what Paul inaugurated—the transition from a Judaeo-Christianity to a Christianity of the Gentiles as such—is not something theologically obvious, but introduces a radically new period of church history, a Christianity that was not an export of Judaeo-Christianity to the Diaspora, but—despite its relatedness to the historical Jesus—a Christianity that grew out of the soil of paganism. I know that all this is vague and not very clear. But I think this is due in the last resort to the fact that the theological problems involved in this transition from Judaeo-Christianity to Gentile Christianity are not at all as simple as people think and that the difficulties have never been properly cleared up. Hence it is not by any means completely clear what Paul 'started' when he declared that circumcision and all that it involved was superfluous for non-Jews (and perhaps only for them).

However this may be, if we want a more precise and truly theological division of church history up to now, it seems to me that the suggested tripartite division is the only right one. It means that the transition from one historical and theological situation into an essentially new one happened only once before in the history of Christianity and is now set to occur for the second time in the transition from the Christianity of Europe (with its American appendages) to an actual world-religion. We can risk making an assertion like this of course only if we regard the transition from the ancient Gentile Christianity of the Mediterranean world to the medieval and modern Christianity of Europe as less theologically incisive than the two caesurae with which we are concerned here. But this seems completely justified in view of the unity of the Roman-Hellenistic Mediterranean culture and its transmission to the Germanic peoples—a unity that need not be examined more closely here.

If what has just been said is at all correct, two questions arise: firstly, in what precisely does the theological and not merely cultural-historical singularity of such a transition, or such a caesura, consist? and secondly, what follows if we apply the theology of this transition to the transition in which we are living today and for which Vatican II was a kind of official ecclesiastical beginning?

So far as the first question is concerned, we can at least say that it refers to an event that is theologically relevant and part of salvation-history, not merely relevant to the history of civilization. This, it seems to me, is obvious from Paul's writings. The abolition of circumcision for Gentile Christians, which he proclaimed—an abolition which Jesus certainly did not foresee and can certainly scarcely be conclusively deduced from his explicit proclamation and from the importance for salvation of his death and resurrection—is for Paul a principle that belongs to his gospel and in some sense a part of revelation; it is an interruption of a continuity of salvation-history which man cannot bring about on his own authority. In this way there arises the theological question properly so called—which even Paul did not sufficiently consider—of what could and must remain from the salvation-history and the Church of the Old Testament if this reality of circumcision, embracing for every Jew the ultimate substance of his existence as oriented to salvation, is abolished and yet—according to Paul—could and should remain for the Jewish Christians of his own time.[1] For him this transition really involved a caesura

---

[1] Cf. Gal. 2:7–10; 1 Cor. 7:17–19; Acts 15:1–29; 21: 18–25.

in the original sense of the term. It should also be remembered that many other abrogations and interruptions in salvation history were linked with this caesura: the abolition of the Sabbath, the transference of the centre of the Church from Jerusalem to Rome, far-reaching modifications in moral teaching, the emergence of new canonical Scriptures with priority over the old, etc. For us here it is unimportant whether these drastic changes can be shown to have the support of Jesus or explicitly only that of Paul or whether they took place otherwise and elsewhere during the apostolic age. Since, even as distinct from patristic and medieval theology, there is no clear and explicitly considered theology of this caesura, of this new beginning of Christianity with Paul as its inaugurator, and since it will have to be worked out gradually only in a dialogue with the Synagogue of today, no one can blame me for not being able to say anything beyond the suggestions already made. And yet I would like to take the risk of putting forward the thesis that today we are for the first time living again in a period of a caesura like that involved in the transition from Judaeo-Christianity to Gentile Christianity.

Is it possible to put forward this thesis and in the light of it explain that Vatican II derives its importance from the fact that it proclaimed—even though only in a rudimentary and vague sort of fashion—a transition from the western Church to the world-Church similar in character to the transition which occurred for the first and only time when the Church ceased to be the Church of the Jews and became the Church of the Gentiles? Once again, I think that this question can be answered in the affirmative. Obviously this does not mean that these two caesurae and transitions are simply alike in their content. No historical event occurs twice. And if someone insists that the caesura inaugurated by Paul has peculiarities also in a formal-theological sense which are not repeated and that therefore the transition to a world-Church is not in every respect comparable to the transition from the Christianity of the Jewish Jesus to the Christianity of Paul, I shall certainly not contradict him. Neither do I doubt that such transitions occur for the most part without premeditation; they are not first thought out and planned in theological terms and only afterwards put into effect, but are realized more or less spontaneously out of a secret instinct of the Spirit and of grace, although what occurs at the same time by way of reflection is not to be despised or regarded as superfluous. With these reservations I would like to affirm and defend this thesis which I put forward.

First of all, I venture to assert that the difference between the historical

situation of Judaeo-Christianity and the situation into which Paul trans-
planted Christianity as in a radically new creation was not greater than
the difference between European culture and the modern cultures of Asia
and Africa as a whole to which Christianity has to be adapted, if it is
really to become the world-Church it has begun to be. The modern
difference may be concealed up to a point by the fact that a stratum of
the rational-industrial culture of Europe and the USA lies above these
other cultures, reducing them to the same level and so disguising the
difference between our culture and the other cultures that it is possible
to gain the impression that Christianity continues to reach any point in
the whole world in the form of a commodity exported from the West and
bringing with it the dubious blessings of the West. But, apart from the
fact that there was a parallel to this in antiquity—the Diaspora of the
Jews with their proselytism (and the phenomenon of the 'God-fearers'
which alone made this possible) in the whole world—on the basis of
which a Judaeo-Christianity might apparently have sent its exports all
over the ancient world, the modern history of the missions shows with
comparatively slight exceptions that Christianity as a western export has
not in practice made any impact on the advanced civilizations of the East
or in the world of Islam. It made no impact because it was western
Christianity and sought to establish itself as such in the rest of the world
without the risk of a really new beginning, breaking with some of the
continuities which had been taken for granted, as was shown in the
various rites controversies, in the export of the Latin liturgical language
into countries where Latin had never been an historical factor, in the way
in which western, Roman law was exported as a matter of course in
Canon Law, in the naive way in which it was taken for granted that the
bourgeois morality of the West could be imposed in every detail on
people of alien cultures, in the rejection of religious experiences of other
cultures, etc. This, then, is the situation: either the Church sees and
recognizes these essential differences of the other cultures, into which it
has to enter as world-Church, and accepts with a Pauline boldness the
necessary consequences of this recognition or it remains a western
Church and thus in the last resort betrays the meaning of Vatican II.

We come to the second question. What is meant more concretely by
making this claim for the significance of Vatican II? It is difficult to say.
For one thing, the second caesura—to the world-Church—has or must
of course have a material content quite different from that of the first,
to the Gentile Church of antiquity and the Middle Ages. For another

thing, the question remains open and unclarified as to whether and how far the Church still retained in the post-apostolic age the creative potential and powers which it had in the period of its first coming-to-be, in apostolic times, and claimed in irreversible or apparently irreversible decisions constituting its concrete nature and going beyond what belonged to it as coming to it directly from Jesus the Risen One himself. The question remains open as to whether with such historical caesurae as this second one the Church can legitimately seize opportunities of which it never made use during its second great epoch, since it would have seemed pointless and therefore illegitimate to do so at the time. The third reason why it is difficult to explain more concretely the importance of the claim that Vatican II marks the transition to the world-Church is that, despite all modern futurology, no one can predict the secular future accurately enough to enable the Church to do justice to it in the new interpretation of its faith and its nature as world-Church. In this sense Vatican II of course provides only a very abstract and formal outline of the task facing the Church as world-Church. Nevertheless, the attempt must be made to say something about the image of the Church as world-Church, about the still outstanding task of the Church. This, I think, is part of the theme of our reflections, since a theological interpretation of the basic nature of Vatican II must be undertaken in the light of its *causa finalis:* that is, of the future of the Church to which this Council was committed.

First of all, we have the Christian proclamation. None of us can say how exactly, with what terminology, under what new aspects, the ancient message of Christianity must be proclaimed in the future in Asia, Africa, the Islamic regions, perhaps also in South America, in order to make this message really present everywhere in the world. The other peoples and cultures must slowly find this out for themselves, although of course we cannot stop at a formal declaration of the necessity of these other proclamations, nor can the latter be deduced from an analysis— itself problematic—of the special characteristics of these peoples. In this task, which is still to be accomplished and which properly speaking is not for us Europeans, it will be necessary to have recourse—while invoking the hierarchy of truths, mentioned by Vatican II—to the basic substance of the Christian message and from that point in spontaneous creativity corresponding to the particular historical situation to formulate again the Church's faith as a whole.

This reduction of the Christian message to its ultimate basic substance as a first step to a fresh statement of the whole content of faith is not easy; it will be necessary in this connection to take advantage of the efforts made in recent years to find basic formularies of faith; but it will also be necessary to raise the question hitherto scarcely considered as to whether there is a formal criterion in the light of which it can be decided what might and what might not be part originally of a supernatural revelation strictly so-called. If this task were fulfilled, there would then be a pluralism of proclamations or, better, the real pluralism which is much more significant than a pluralism of proclamations and theologies within the western Church. Since in principle all men can talk with all others and can reach agreement with one another, these plural proclamations would not simply be disparate factors. They could mutually criticize and enrich each other, but everyone of them would nevertheless have an historical individuality which in the last resort would be incommensurable with any other. Hence the question emerges as to how a unity of faith can be maintained and established together with a plurality of proclamations, how the Church's supreme authority in Rome could work towards this end, since it is obviously a task quite different from that undertaken hitherto by the Roman authorities on faith against a common European background of understanding.

It has frequently been observed that a similar pluralism of liturgies is required, which cannot consist merely in the use of different vernacular languages. Quite apart from the fact that genuine progress towards unity in the ecumenical question cannot otherwise be expected, it is really quite obvious that a considerable pluralism with reference to Canon Law (and also the rest of the Church's practice) must be developed in the larger particular churches. All these of course are formal, abstract statements which say little about the concrete shape of the future world-Church. But is it possible to say something more?

We have reached the conclusion. All our reflections were meant to deal with the question of how the Second Vatican Council is to be theologically interpreted. We tried to make clear why it was the event in church history in which the world-Church began hesitatingly to act as such. With a few problematical reflections we tried to make clear that the coming-to-be of the world-Church as such does not mean merely a quantitative augmentation of the earlier Church, but contains a theological caesura in church history which has not by any means been clearly considered, which can be compared perhaps only with the transition from Judaeo-Christianity to Gentile Christianity, the caesura which occupied Paul, although we do not need to think that he had given adequate theological consideration to this transition of which he was the protagonist. This is all that really had to be said. Everything else has been examined only vaguely, perhaps developed very unsystematically and without clarity; problems scarcely considered in traditional theology have only been indicated here.

In closing, attention may be drawn to a peculiarity of Vatican II with which I have dealt elsewhere and into which I cannot now enter at greater length. At least in *Gaudium et Spes* the Council adopted spontaneously a mode of expression which had the character neither of dogmatic teaching valid for all time nor of canonical enactments, but was perhaps to be understood as the expression of 'instructions' or 'appeals' (presupposing a theory about official ecclesiastical statements which is not yet by any means explicit, since in this respect we are familiar only with *dogmatic* statements and official ecclesiastical *enactments* and orders). Will this new mode of expression acquire a greater importance in the future? Under what conditions can such instructions be made effective? These too are questions into which we cannot enter more closely here, although their investigation might help us from another angle to answer the question of the specifically theological character of this Council.

Finally there is something that can be expressly stated or repeated. Together with and under the Pope, the Council was the active subject of the supreme powers in the Church in whatever direction these powers are exercised. This is obvious, it was expressly taught, nor was it actually questioned by Paul VI. But how this supreme power, whose holders are the Pope 'alone' *and* the Council, can exist in and be exercised by two at least partially different subjects, has not become really clear in theory, nor is it clear in practice what is permanently relevant in the fact that the whole college of bishops with and under the Pope—but actually *with* the Pope—is the supreme collegial governing body of the Church. Up to now the permanent relevance of this principle of the collegial constitution of the Church has not been clear and was thrust into the background after the Council by Paul VI. Will John Paul II change anything in this respect? In a real world-Church something of the kind is necessary, since a world-Church simply cannot be ruled by that Roman centralism which was usual in the time of Pius XII.

7

THE ABIDING SIGNIFICANCE OF THE SECOND VATICAN COUNCIL

HAS THE Second Vatican Council a lasting significance? This is a question already being raised today, often with some embarrassment and a kind of resignation, by Christians to whom the Church still means something. Before attempting to answer this question, we may begin with a few preliminary observations.

At the moment when it occurs, every historical event is clouded over, accompanied by contradictory feelings, by a variety of expectations and apprehensions, often arbitrary and fanciful, and is contrary to the interpretation of contemporaries. All this of course fades very quickly, but has nothing to do with the question of the true significance of an historical event. Napoleon's significance is still a factor of our history even today, although explicitly it rouses the curiosity only of specialist historians and scarcely anyone else ever mentions it.

The question of the significance of a council can be raised with reference to the Church as a whole or it can be a question referring to an individual regional church. The two questions are not identical. If the question of the meaning of the Council for a particular regional church is one that frequently necessitates a negative answer, this may be sad for the regional church, but it is in no way prejudicial to the Church as a whole.

The answer to our basic question may be given in the indicative, but in the last resort it is an imperative, addressed to the Church of today and tomorrow. Such an imperative implies prognoses, expectations, apprehensions, which at present can only be somewhat uncertainly conjectured. Behind our basic question lies the conviction that this Council brought to the future Church new tasks and new challenges to which reactions must still be expected. If this is so, then in any case the Council has a great importance, since a task is there which becomes a blessing or a judgement for us and for the future generation, depending on whether we cope with the task or not. If this Council presents us with a task of this kind (and I am sure it does), then the Council has a meaning. It then belongs not merely to the past, but is present now—as the herald of a task for the future. I would like to suggest the following thesis for the theological interpretation of the Council, in order to use it as the starting point for answering the essential question.

COUNCIL OF THE WORLD-CHURCH

Without disputing previous initiatives, the Council seems to me to be the first act in a history in which the world-Church first began to exist as such. In the nineteenth and twentieth centuries the Church moved slowly and tentatively from being a potential to becoming an actual world-Church, from being a European and western Church with European exports to the whole world to becoming a world-Church which is present, albeit in very varied degrees of intensity, in the whole world and no longer merely as a European and North American export. Everywhere it has a native clergy, now aware of their autonomy and responsibility. This world-Church acted in the Council for the first time in historical clarity in the dimension of doctrine and law.

The Council was a council of the world-Church as such, even though it cannot be denied that the European and North American regional churches largely predominated. The simplest proof of this obvious and yet unprecedented and unique fact is that the responsibility for this Council—as distinct from all previous councils, not excepting Vatican I—was in the hands of an episcopate from the whole world and not merely, as at the First Vatican Council, an episcopate of European missionary bishops exported to the whole world.

This thesis is not really to be proved here, nor will its meaning be developed; it is meant only as an aid to answering our own question. That is to say, if we start out from this thesis, we do not need *a priori* to ask from a narrow intra-European standpoint what is there new that the Council has brought to us (in fact, a great deal), but we have to ask what is the permanent significance of this Council as a council of the world-Church. It is then again obvious that this significance by way of repercussion is also a significance for a European regional church and that questions may be raised also in this connection.

We may begin with the fact that the Council was the cause of the abolition of Latin as the common liturgical language. We can safely say that without the Council Latin would still be the liturgical language throughout the world. We need not be prophets to say that this change can never be reversed. Nor is this situation changed at all by the fact that, for the time being, the basic pattern set up in Rome for the regional vernacular liturgies is itself in Latin. In the light of the Church's unity and the theological continuity of Christian worship there will always be an ultimate liturgical unity behind the regional liturgies. But, as a result of the diversity of liturgical languages, there will be a necessary and irreversible process of development of a variety of liturgies, even though it is impossible to predict with certainty and accuracy the relationship between similarity and diversity of the regional liturgies. In the long run the liturgy of the Church as a whole will not simply be the liturgy of the Roman church in translation, but a unity in the variety of regional liturgies, each of which will have its own peculiar character which will not consist merely in its language.

If however the nature of the Church and consequently the nature and peculiar character of a regional church is also derived substantially from the liturgy in which it finds its supreme actualizations, then the result will be the formation of truly autonomous regional churches which are more than administrative districts of a totally and homogeneously organized state; these will emerge from the development of autonomous liturgies which began with the replacement of the Latin liturgical language by the national languages. Of course it will not be possible to think of these slowly emerging liturgies simply in the light of the pattern of the ancient Near East. The new liturgies do not need to deny their historical descent from the Roman liturgy. It cannot yet be predicted how great their differences will be.

RELATIONSHIP TO THE WORLD

In several decrees—among which the Pastoral Constitution on the Church in the Modern World *(Gaudium et Spes)* and the Declaration on Religious Freedom are especially important—the Church attempted to describe its fundamental relationship to the secular world, which arises from its own nature and is not imposed on it by external circumstances. What was said there about renouncing external means of power in matters of religion, about the respect due even to an erroneous conscience, about the development of a legitimately secular world outside the Church's control, at first came up against a certain amount of stubborn resistance on the part of conservative groups at the Council and could be regarded as exceptional, as a statement forced by a secular world on the Church contrary to the latter's innermost feelings or as objectifications of the outlook of liberal-minded Christians but not as objectifications of Christianity itself.

If however we remember that, even where it has or could have a greater power in the secular sphere, the Church now must observe the restraint of which it spoke at the Council, since this is required by its very nature, although in its history this requirement was only too often disregarded on the plea that to do so was to render a service to God; if we remember also that the temptation may arise again and again, albeit in new forms and shapes, for the Church to abandon this restraint wholly or partially, but that in principle and generally the post-conciliar Church can no longer yield to this temptation, then it can be perceived that something permanent has come to be through the Council. Individual churches, individual bishops and militant laymen in particular may be repeatedly faced with the temptation to use means of power to impose on non-Christians what is really or supposedly true and helpful to salvation in Christianity and the Church, and here and there they will yield to it. But, while the power politicians (in the most sublime sense of the word) in the Church could act with a clear conscience in a clerical-fascist way before the Council, because—as they said—falsehood and evil have no rights and can at most be tactically tolerated, such trends can now be condemned and opposed in the name of Christianity itself. According to the decrees of the Council, it is no longer so easy to give a Christian *façade* to the restriction of freedom in the name of what is claimed to be alone good and right.

Of course that is not to say that these decrees of the Council can be interpreted only in this way. But the importance of this interpretation can be seen from a glance at the trends in modern Islamic states. There attempts are being made to set up an ecclesiastical polity or a theocracy in which the Koran is the basic law of the state and twenty strokes of the whip is the punishment for not fasting during the month of Ramadan. Are we as Christians merely too sluggish or too cowardly to attempt something of the kind in our own milieu? Would we do it if we could? Or do we refrain from such religious power-politics as a matter of principle, even though it might still be possible, at least in small doses.

In this respect too the Second Vatican Council is still relevant and sets us a task. As the Council says, for the sake of the common weal, it will never be possible to do without force and power; we Christians are under no obligation here to chase after unreal Utopias. But in principle the Church at the Council surrendered a good deal of power that it had formerly assumed, whenever possible, as a matter of course. At this point a frontier has been crossed behind which it will never again be possible to return, even to a slight degree.

THEOLOGY OF THE COUNCIL

Theology at the Council was in a transitional situation that was difficult to define. On the one hand neoscholastic theology was taken for granted. It predominated to an almost alarming extent in the drafts prepared for the Council by the Roman commissions. In these, among other doctrines proposed for definition, were the descent of all human beings from a single couple (monogenism) and 'limbo' as the destiny of unbaptized children: theologoumena which today have almost entirely disappeared. At the Council Latin predominated as the language in which this neoscholastic theology was expressed, the New Testament being used as a collection of proof-texts while little or no attempt was made to bring a biblical theology to bear on the problems. This was one aspect of the Council's theology. It should not however be inferred that this aspect was merely obscure and negative. On the contrary, one could wish that students of theology even today were a little more aware of the conceptual exactitude of neoscholasticism and of its orientation to declarations of the magisterium.

There was however another aspect of the Council's theology. It was more biblical than neoscholasticism. It had proposed, a little timidly and cautiously, themes which had not been drawn simply from the repertoire of neoscholasticism. It exercised a moderating influence on any sort of theological exuberance (for example, in Mariology). As far as possible, it made an effort to take ecumenical needs into account: something which had not hitherto been taken for granted in Rome, not even under the level-headed and judicious Pius XI. It was convinced that it is possible to say something that is theologically important without solemnly proclaiming it as a dogma. In the field of dogmatic theology properly socalled it brought more clearly to the fore of the Church's awareness a series of doctrines which in themselves were not really new or unprecedented or particularly controversial, but which had not previously been stated clearly enough to make an impact on the practical life of the Church. Among these may be mentioned the sacramentality of episcopal ordination, the doctrine of the episcopate as a whole (with and under the Pope) as the supreme ecclesiastical authority in regard to proclaiming the faith and in matters of law, the doctrine that the human authors of Scripture were not secretaries of the God who inspired them but truly human composers of these Scriptures, the cautious formulation of the inerrancy of Scripture, and many another theme that cannot be listed individually here.

The theology of the Council has two aspects. It is the theology of a transition. The question remains of course whether, how and how rapidly this theology will continue to develop after acquiring a certain official authorization at the Council. The theology acquired and proclaimed after the Council by the Roman Congregation for the Doctrine of the Faith may perhaps still show some traces of the influence of conciliar theology, but it is too neoscholastic in its nervous opposition to modern theological experiments, too nervous and too little creative in regard to the questions with which modern theology is occupied. The theology of the Congregation of the Doctrine of the Faith is a defensive theology, warning and prohibiting, but not really succeeding in justifying its prohibitions and warnings (which, as such, are perhaps not always unjustified or superfluous) in the light of a living and broad coherence of faith as a whole, in a way that renders them intelligible to anyone who is prepared to think and live by this totality of faith. But the Congregation for the Doctrine of the Faith need not remain for ever as it is now and it will not be able to lead back the theology of the Church as a whole behind the frontier crossed at the Council, even though the crossing was more or less unpremeditated. Of course only tasks and hopes can be formulated here and no prophecies can be made, particularly since signs of fatigue can be detected in the theology of the last ten years: an escape into pastoral studies and religious educational theory or to a false anthropocentrism which closes man up in himself.

Theology however will go on living, renewing continually its strength and vitality. Corresponding to the Council itself, it will become a world-theology: that is, it will exist in the non-European, non-North American countries, but no longer merely as an export from the West. Latin America has already staked its claim to a theology of its own. 'Theology of Liberation' is not the only title that might be given to such an autonomous Latin American theology. Perhaps Africa also and the Far East will soon develop theologies of a specific character as a result of coming to terms creatively with their own cultures. That however is no reason why we in the West should abandon our own efforts on these lines.

It is not as if the theology of the West no longer had any function, and not only because theology necessarily has a function as long as history continues and as long therefore as new situations continue to emerge and to require a new proclamation of the Christian faith. Even today the theology of the West has a quite incalculable back-log to make up. It has to be a missionary theology; it cannot think and speak merely in the assured, traditional forms, addressing those who still feel at home in Christianity and in the Church; it must direct its thinking to the others to whom, for a variety of reasons, Christianity has become something alien. At every step, then, it must be dogmatic and fundamental theology in one. In the West it could certainly accomplish some preliminary work for the theologies of the rest of the world, even though these are expected to be autonomous, since the West with its enlightenment and technological rationality is becoming increasingly involved in the destiny of the rest of the world.

It cannot be our task here to describe exactly this theology of the future, the demands on it, its novelty, and so on. It may however be said that the Council made a new start possible and legitimate. Because of the Council and after it, theology of itself no longer presents the appearance of a monotonous neoscholasticism intended to be acceptable in the whole world. Neither is it any longer the case that every more intelligent candidate for the priesthood and the episcopal office, coming from what have been known as the missionary countries, must study in Rome and there be initiated with all the others into one and the same neoscholasticism. Theology will be everywhere in the world-Church and it will inevitably have to deal with the more urgent questions in any particular cultural group and which are not now the same everywhere. And the resultant, undeniable diversity will make its mark on the specific character of theology as a whole. It is obvious that the Roman magisterium will consequently have different tasks and have to develop modes of procedure other than those of the times when it had to address as a matter of course a single cultural group. Whether this prospect is sufficiently clearly seen is another question.

ECUMENICAL CHANGE OF MIND

The Council represents a caesura in the history of the relations of the Catholic Church both with other Christian Churches and communities and with non-Christian world-religions. Of course the Church's sense of faith at all times implied convictions which in the last resort and in principle authorized the newly established relationship of the Catholic Church with other Christian Churches and communities and with the non-Christian religions. But formerly these convictions had no effect on this relationship. Non-Christians were regarded simply as living in the darkness of paganism and assured of salvation only through the preaching of the gospel. Non-Catholic Christendom was seen as a whole as a mass of heretics who were to be invited either in a friendly or threatening way to be converted and to return to the one true Catholic Church, without any thought that this return to unity might also carry with it important changes in the Catholic Church itself.

It is not at all easy to create a theological awareness of the caesura resulting from the Council. The theological reasons for the caesura were indeed present at an earlier stage: the assumption of God's universal salvific will in Christ, the doctrine of the opportunity of salvation without sacraments, of the implicit desire of membership of the Church, of the validity of baptism even outside the Catholic Church, and so on. These ever-present theological truisms might give the impression that nothing has really changed in the relationship between the Church and the rest of mankind. On the other hand, the Catholic theologian, as distinct from the disinterested non-theologian, cannot take the new closeness and the positive relationship between the Christian denominations and the relationship of Christianity to the non-Christian religions to mean that there are no serious differences, divisions and tasks in the way of unification, as if the Catholic Church were simply any kind of structure resulting from historical chance, among the many others of more or less equal importance produced by the history of religion or the history of the Church. These two difficulties, to right and left, make it difficult to see the change that began with the Second Vatican Council and is now irreversible. We shall try to throw some light on this change, even though this means perhaps saying too much for some and too little for others.

Christianity has always maintained that there is a true history of revelation and of faith in which what happens is not always the same but includes new, far-reaching changes. With the event of Jesus Christ of course the history of revelation reached an unsurpassable peak and an unparalleled irreversibility, which are not to be disguised or minimized here. But the Church's sense of faith does not cease to be an historical reality following a single track and with far-reaching caesurae, even though this is not made clear in the usual theory of the history of dogma, which has hitherto interpreted the development of dogma as a matter of logical deduction from the original data of revelation. If we ask what the Council has produced that is new in this one-track, irreversible progress, the main answer must be that at this Council, Catholic Christendom adopted expressly a different, a new attitude toward other Christians and their Churches and toward the non-Christian world-religions and ratified it as truly Christian.

The decisive thing about this ecumenical change of mind in the widest sense of the term lies in the fact that the greatness and radicality of this change are concealed and minimized in our ordinary consciousness by a modern, liberal and relativistic mentality which from the very outset regards the new ecumenical openness and readiness to learn as simply to be taken for granted. People like this see what happened in this respect at the Council as nothing really important or as merely obvious; the Council merely noted what had long been a matter of course outside a clerical-ecclesiastical ghetto. Nor can it be denied that, historically speaking, this modern liberalist mentality was in fact the climate in which alone the new ecumenical awareness could grow. Nevertheless, this awareness grew from genuinely Christian roots and is as such Christian. It definitively abandons an older mentality, which prevailed for fifteen hundred years, and remains obligatory for the future of the Church, like other great events in the history of faith.

All in all, without denying that the seeds of the future were already present in the past, it has to be said that, before the Council, the Catholic Church regarded the non-Roman Catholic Churches and communities as organizations of heretics, as societies of human beings differing from the old Church only by their errors and defects and needing to return to it, in order to find there the whole truth and fullness of Christianity. For the old view, the non-Christian religions as a whole were no more than the terrible darkness of paganism, all that man in his sin and without grace could produce from his own resources by way of religion. That in an ecumenical unification the non-Catholic Churches might also bring with them to the one Church of the future a positive heritage from the history of Christianity in a form not known in the old Church; that the non-Christian religions even in their institutional form might exercise a positive salvific function for non-Christian humanity: none of this was actually explicit in the Church's awareness, but is present there now and can never again be excluded, since it is understood, not as a liberal mentality of modern times, but as an element of the Christian outlook as such.

Once again, no one who maintains in principle the radical differences between truth and error, who has recognized a true claim to absoluteness on the part of Christianity and the Church, who grants in principle to certain formulated insights and religious institutions a significance that has a part in deciding man's eternal destiny, can regard the caesura which came in with the Council as something to be taken for granted. He must recognize it as a fundamentally Christian event, as a victory of Christianity and not of liberalism. He must be prepared to put up with and work on all the theological problems involved in such a change—something that is not at all easy and will remain as a task for a long time.

OPTIMISM OF UNIVERSAL SALVATION

The implications of the above brief suggestions may be investigated more deeply and more radically, in order to see—despite the lack of interest of so many Christians—what this Council means for the Church. Even though the enormous variety of his theology means that we may be doing Augustine an injustice by the following description, even though the fact cannot be overlooked that the history of the Church's sense of faith has continued in many small steps from him to us, even though, as we have said, many historical causes have co-operated as catalysts in this change in the Church's sense of faith, nevertheless it can be said that Augustine inaugurated and taught to Christendom a view of world-history according to which—in the incomprehensibility of God's providence—world-history remained the history of the *massa damnata* from which in the last resort, by a rarely granted grace of election, only a few were saved. For him the world was dark and only weakly illuminated by the light of God's grace, a grace that can be seen by its rarity to be unmerited. Even though Augustine from time to time showed that he was aware of the presence in the Church of many who seemed to be outside it and vice-versa, nevertheless for him the group of those who are saved and enter into glory is more or less identical with the community of those who believe explicitly in Christianity and the Church. As a result of an incomprehensibly just judgement of God, the rest remain in the *massa damnata* of humanity, and on the whole the outcome of world-history is to be found in hell.

This pessimism of Augustine in regard to salvation was reconstructed and slowly transformed in an inexpressibly wearisome process in the Church's theoretical and existential consciousness. From the assumption that unbaptized children are tormented by the fires of hell to the abolition by modern theologians of limbo—although a draft prepared for the Council still tried to maintain this doctrine—was a very long way. But all these insights, acquired bit by bit, leading to an optimistic view of the prospect of salvation, a salvation which could be prevented only by the evil will of the individual and which might still be hoped for in virtue of the power of grace transforming this malice again into a free love of God, these insights the Church had not ratified and taught absolutely firmly before the Council.

The Council however says that even someone who regards himself as an atheist, if only he follows his conscience, is united to the paschal mystery of Christ; that every human being in a way known only to God is in touch with God's revelation and can really believe by an act that is salutary in a theological sense. There too it is said that even those who seek the unknown God in shadows and images are not far from the true God, who wills all men to be saved if they only strive to lead a righteous life. The Council also stressed the fact that the Church is not so much the community only of those who are saved as the sacramental primordial sign and germ-cell of salvation for the whole world.

Of course it could be said that this optimism of the Council in regard to universal salvation also remains hypothetical, that it could break down as a result of an individual's final culpability, that in this hypothetical way it was the normal teaching of the Church even before the Council. It is indeed true that even after the Council the Church has not proclaimed any doctrine of universal reconciliation *(apocatastasis)* and before it had also taught God's universal salvific will. But this preconciliar teaching was understood in a very abstract way and qualified with not a few ifs and buts, which cannot be maintained after the Council. The Council tacitly buried the doctrine of 'limbo' for children dying before baptism; it boldly postulated a revelation properly so called, and consequently a real opportunity of faith even where the Christian message had not been proclaimed; it did not regard even the profession of atheism as an unambiguous proof that a person could not be saved—which certainly is not in agreement with the traditional teaching before the Council.

There are other points that should also be remembered. It can be said that in theory and also largely in religious practice those were regarded in the first place as culpable (if not absolutely condemned) who were objectively opposed to Christianity and the Church, at least if they could not be counted among religious 'primitives'. This sort of attitude was not so unintelligible then as it seems today. If, according to the teaching of Vatican I, there are clear, unequivocal arguments, adapted to all times and people, for the existence of God, for revelation and for the divine foundation of the Church, then it was not too difficult to conclude that a person could reject these arguments only culpably, and consequently that the culpability of heretics and non-Christians had to be assumed from the start.

Certainly there can be no talk of such an assumption in the decrees of Vatican II and in all that happened in connection with the Council. The Pope embraces non-Catholic church leaders and pagans; a Roman cardinal declared in Tunis that Mohammed had been a true prophet; all ecumenical conversations assume that all the partners to the discussion are living in the grace of God. Although rejecting a theoretical doctrine of universal reconciliation, the Church in the Council and in its practical conduct starts out from the assumption that God's grace is not only offered to man's free decision, but also that it largely prevails universally in this freedom. This attitude of the Church came into existence of course only after a very long period of development. But it became clear and irreversible in the Second Vatican Council; for such a hope can certainly grow, while it can no longer really decline.

Formerly theology asked apprehensively, how many are saved from the *massa damnata* of world-history. Today we ask whether we may hope that all are saved. This question, this attitude, is more Christian than the former and is the fruit of a more mature Christian awareness that has grown over a long period and is slowly coming to terms more closely with the ultimate basic message of Jesus on the victory of God's Kingdom. It is an attitude which may seem obvious to the liberalistic, bourgeois philistine, since he knows nothing of the incomprehensibility of God's judgements and of his all-consuming holiness and consequently thinks that the message of the victory of God's grace in the world is something that God might perhaps use to justify himself before man's tribunal. But if someone has even a remote idea of who God is, is really aware of the terrible darkness of the history of humanity, he will find the optimism of universal salvation which the Church has struggled to acquire an almost frightening message to which he has to respond with the ultimate resources of his faith.

At the beginning, we put forward the thesis that this Council was the first great official action of a world-Church that had now become relevant. The world-Church as such has appeared on the scene and it now tells the world—inexplicably marvellous and yet taken for granted—that, with all the depths of its history and all the grim possibilities of its future, it is embraced by God and his will, through whose unfathomable love God himself in his self-communication offers himself to the world as ground, power and goal, and of himself makes this offer effective in the freedom of history. The Church became new at this Council, since it had become a world-Church and as such it gives the world a message which, although always the heart of the message of Jesus, is today proclaimed more unconditionally and courageously than formerly and therefore in a new way. In both respects, in the messenger and his message, something new has happened, something irreversible, something that remains. It is another question, whether, in the dull mediocrity of our activity in the Church, we seize and live here and now on this new reality. But this is our task.

8

THE FUTURE OF THE CHURCH
AND THE CHURCH OF THE FUTURE

I F WE are to speak of the Church's future, the obvious question
arises as to which Church is meant. Is it the Catholic Church
in our own country? The western Church? Or the world-Church
as a whole? It must be made clear from the outset that these three
questions are different and that the answer to each of them is not necessarily the same. It might, for example, be necessary to take a very
pessimistic view of the future of Christianity in our own country and in
Europe, while at the same time seeing the future of the world-Church
of South America and Africa in a very different light. At any rate these
three questions must be distinguished. Here, in what must be only a brief
reflection, we shall look mainly to the world-Church as a whole and its
future; in other words, we shall not be concerned, properly speaking and
expressly, with prognoses in regard to our own country, our own native
land, or to Europe. If then we are dealing with the world-Church and
its future as a whole, we must be content with very general considerations
and cannot at the same time analyse more exactly the sociopolitical
situation of individual countries and continents and its possible effect on
the future of the Church. We assume that our interest in the future of
the world-Church will not really distract us from our concern and hopes
for the Church in our own country but will reveal a horizon within which
alone it is possible to understand correctly this concern and these hopes.

We are speaking here of the future of our Church, of the Roman
Catholic Church. But this does not mean raising subliminally and tacitly
the question of the opportunities open to our Church in competition with
other Christian Churches and communities. This is not the meaning of
our chosen theme. As long as the Christian Churches have not achieved

complete unity, they are inevitably in competition and present contrasts with each other and one Church's opportunities for the future are not necessarily equal to those of another Church in the same country. But this is not what concerns us here. Even though we are talking about the Roman Catholic Church and its future, our interest lies in this Church as a part of Christendom as one and whole, we are really looking to the future of Christianity as a whole in the secularized world of today, in which all Christian Churches have to live: in the world of a rational, technical civilization; in a world where the individual parts are increasingly growing together into a unity and a common destiny; in a world which, as never before, is marked by a militant atheism, not as a private influence, but as a world-wide public power. If then we refer explicitly here to the Catholic Church and its future, in the last resort we are looking in an ecumenical spirit to Christendom in its unity and wholeness and to its future.

If we are to speak of the future of the world-Church, we can do so only in the light of an understanding of its *nature* that is based on faith and theologically correct. In its ultimate nature the Church is the sociologically and historically tangible and structured community of those who believe in Jesus Christ crucified and risen as the definitive and victoriously prevailing self-promise of the one and living God to the world. Hence this Church is the basic sacrament of the salvation of the world: of the world, and not only of those who belong to the Church itself expressly and in a sociologically tangible way. The Church is the historically perceptible assurance of the victory of God's self-promise as the ultimate meaning and absolute future of the world. To this world the Church promises God's salvation, a salvation that will be realized by God's mysterious grace even where the Church itself has not been established visibly in its word and its sacraments. It is to this very world that the grace of God is offered and attested as victorious by the Church. If the Church is thus the sacrament of salvation for the non-ecclesial world, that is not to say of course that those may remain aloof from the Church who have been offered the grace of belonging to the Church and are expected, as a result of their publicly professed faith in Jesus Christ as God's one and definitive promise of salvation to the world, to take their part in sustaining the Church as basic sacrament: to remain aloof would imperil their eternal salvation.

This essential task of the Church, which has been merely outlined here, is of the utmost importance for a correct understanding of the future of the Church. As a result of the history of the Church over two thousand years, devout churchgoing Christians have been misled into thinking of the future history of the Church as one of ever-increasing numerical growth, not only in an absolute sense, but also relatively to the numbers of the human race as a whole. This feeling about the future of the Church, originating in its past history, was highly problematic even formerly, if only because the size, historical weight and future of non-Christian humanity outside Europe at that time had not really seriously been.taken into account. However that may be, as Christians today, we must certainly allow for the fact that the Church will increase numerically in an absolute sense in the future, but will decrease and become smaller by comparison with the numbers of the human race as a whole. This will come about simply because of the more rapid growth of non-Christian peoples, quite apart from the progressive de-Christianization of formerly Christian nations and the consequences of a state-supported militant atheism. But this probably correct prognosis does not do away with the fact that the Church in the last hundred and fifty years, from being a Church of the West, of the purely European civilization and its colonial exports, has gradually become really a world-Church which is present to a varying extent in all parts of the world and everywhere becoming a genuine element of all cultures and nations. The decline relatively to the total population of the Church and Christianity as a whole, now beginning, does not eliminate the coming-to-be and the being of the world-Church as such. Today more than ever it is present everywhere as the basic sacrament of the salvation of the world, a fact however that must not lead us to forget or to assume that we can leave unanswered, for instance, the obscure question of the situation of China as representing a quarter of mankind as a whole.

If we clearly realize the essentially theological nature of the Church as the basic sacrament of salvation, promising salvation to the world and not merely to itself, if in our modern ecclesiology we prefer the metaphor of the basic sacrament to the older metaphor of the Church as the sole ark of salvation on the sea of a perishing world, then we can look more impartially to the future. The Church is everywhere: in the last resort its nature and its function remain independent of the question of its numerical relationship to the total world-population.

This reminder to take a realistic and not a triumphalist view of the Church's future—based on theological grounds and not merely the expression of a momentary defeatism—must not lead us to assume that the prospects are dim for the Church historically and in the mental climate of the world of the future. If in 1973 695 million Catholics formed 18.3 percent of the population of the world, if in this Church alone in some 230 thousand parishes in more than two thousand dioceses about 420 thousand priests were proclaiming the gospel, if, for example, in Africa even now there are 44 million Catholics, in Central and South America about 270 million and in Asia 56 million Catholics (even though only 2.5 percent of these are Asians), if we remember the 320 million Catholics in Europe and North America, if in addition we accept the many hundreds of millions of non-Catholic Christians as parts of the one Christendom, then it can and must be said that the Catholic Church and still more Christendom as a whole represent a world-wide historically and sociologically powerful reality which cannot be left out of account even for a purely worldly and secular prognosis for later centuries. Nor is this secular prognosis invalidated by the fact that enormous numbers of these Catholics and Christians are only nominally such and are only very loosely attached to the Church and Christianity. It is the sort of thing that is found, not only in the Churches, but with all historical and sociological forces which claim to have a mission to mankind and to a more distant future. Even in the 'Churches' of materialism and militant atheism a large number are uninterested fellow-travellers or count as members merely sociologically and statistically. And yet these numbers have some importance for the future in all historical and sociological groups. In the light merely of the numerical size of the Church and of Christianity as a whole, it can still be said that the latter will remain— even in a secular estimate of future possibilities—significant factors in mankind for an unforeseeable period.

For the real Christian, however, such reflections are essentially provisional and external. The real Christian judges the future opportunities of the Church and Christianity from quite a different standpoint, that of faith in the proper sense of the term and of hope that is given by God. For the churchgoing Christian, faith and hope are constitutive elements of his relationship to the Church itself. He does not come to the Church from outside with the question of the future, as to a factor distinct from himself, in order to ask in a neutral spirit about its future possibilities. In fact, with an absolute decision of his free existence, he believes in God as his own eternal life and in Jesus Christ as the historical seal by his victorious power of God's self-promise to the world. And if the Christian believes and hopes in this way and does so together with others through whose mediation he receives the message of God and of Jesus Christ, he is setting up the Church by this very faith and hope in God's victory. The Christian thus affirms the Church with that absolute, unconditional decision with which in faith and hope he reaches out for God in Jesus Christ. The Church itself is the object of Christian faith. And, just as in the last resort the content of faith as a whole is not affirmed by individual human considerations, devious or straightforward, but by the comprehensive basic act of existence in which this whole existence is trustfully surrendered in the light of Jesus' victorious death to the incomprehensible mystery of God, so hope in the future of the Church in the last resort is exalted in this faith above everything and independently of secular futurological considerations and calculations.

Since the Christian sets up and grasps unconditionally and unreservedly the hope of his own salvation (hoping against hope, as Paul says) and since this hope includes the affirmation of the Church, since he has the same absolute hope for the Church's future, it does not matter for him whether the prognoses for the future of the Church, from a purely human standpoint, are favourable or unfavourable. Since the Christian may not, will not and does not despair of his own salvation, neither can he despair of the Church, since this salvific faith itself—if it is rightly understood and is revealed in its whole nature—continually renews the Church about whose future he might have been tempted to doubt. From this standpoint the Christian can also look into the history of faith and perceive there, in what is truly the history of the Church itself, the continual recurrence of phases and moments at which, humanly speaking, there was a strong temptation to predict the decline of the Church and after which again and again everything went on as before. A similar scrutiny of the history of faith might begin with ancient Israel which, considered in the light of secular history, ought long ago to have vanished from the historical scene and yet continues to live by its invincible faith. Likewise, a glance at the history of faith could reveal over and over again in the two thousand years of the Church's history situations in which, humanly speaking, it seemed impossible that everything would continue as before, when it seemed that the end had really come.

Again, however, over and above such empirical assurances, drawn from the history of faith and of the Church, the Christian believes by an ultimate decision of faith, rooted in the depths of his existence, that the Church will exist also in the future. For he believes in God, who grants to man's existence an infinite dignity and an eternal life through his radical fall into death; he believes in Jesus Christ who, by his death, reaches this eternal life as the Risen One and thus definitively seals our hope. But when the Christian believes in this way, it is always an event of the Church; if he so believes and hopes for himself and his salvation, he simply cannot fail to be hoping also for the coming generations: that is, he is sure that these too, believing and hoping, by the power of God's grace, will seize on their salvation and so form the Church, the community of those who with Jesus place their hope in God himself. In the last resort, the future of the Church is not a theme for secular futurology, but an object of the faith that relies unconditionally on God himself.

If we are to talk about the future of the Church, we must not say simply that it has a future; we must also ask whether and how, even at the present time, we can know something about the content and the essential character of this future.

First of all, with reference to this new question, it must be said that, if we are thinking of longer periods of time, we know little or nothing about the character of this future. Even the prediction of the future course of secular world history by philosophers of history, sociologists and futurologists, is a highly problematic business. Today we can certainly say quite a lot about how technical civilization can be expected to develop; we can perhaps estimate more or less accurately the size of the population of the world in the year 2000. But, even from the viewpoint of secular history, at bottom we know nothing about what the Church will look like really concretely in a few decades. In the history of nature and particularly of freedom there are too many unknowns, with all the unforeseeable feed-back effects even of the known factors, for us to be able really to know what the world will be like concretely in fifty years' time. This unforeseeability of future history is particularly relevant to the Church. We cannot form any concrete picture of its future. For, in the first place, we know too little and nothing at all concrete about the secular future. But it is on this as the situation of the Church and its history that the Church's future largely depends. If the course of secular history runs into a future that cannot be clarified in advance, this is even more true of the Church's future. Moreover, the future history of the Church as history of faith and salvation is always governed also by God's freedom and man's freedom, effecting salvation or disaster, whether we think of this freedom of God and man in the history of salvation and consequently of the Church as effective through secular causes or in addition to these.

This unforeseeability of the Church's concrete future may not however be understood properly as an unfortunate impediment for someone who wants to move into a future calculated in advance as accurately as possible. The unforeseeability of future history is in fact a condition of the possibility of true freedom which produces what is original and underivable—since this is unique—and brings to the light the future by itself and not by an advance calculation; it is in particular a condition of the possibility of faith properly so called, which surrenders itself regardless of detailed calculations and unconditionally to God's incomprehensibility and his freedom. The incalculability of the Church's future is part of its nature and that of faith. Anyone who really believes regards this situation in the last resort, not as menacing or intimidating, but as natural and obvious. Faith can make its way into the unfathomable, since all individual unfathomabilities of history are surpassed from the outset by the unfathomable incomprehensibility of God and his freedom itself, which faith as such seeks to grasp.

Even though we cannot know anything about the substance of the Church's concrete future, two statements at least may be made about this future, since on the one hand it is *history* and on the other the history of one and the same enduring Church. That is to say: the Church's future will be different in many respects from the present, in which we ourselves live and which we therefore know. Nevertheless, the future is that of the one and enduring Church in which we believe and live. Change and endurance belong equally to the nature of the Church, while it is obvious that we cannot distinguish so completely in human reflection the changeable from the permanent in this historical factor as to know in advance of its concrete history precisely and conceptually where the dividing line lies between the perishing and the permanent: we must always experience in history the unforeseeable miracle that the Church changes to a quite unforeseeable extent and yet discover that it has remained the same.

Assuming all this, we can safely say that the Church of the future will look very different from that of today. In this respect we must remember that, for the most varied reasons, the tempo of history has enormously increased and consequently that a human being in his very brief life-time now experiences with joy and even more with pain, and with increasing insecurity, more changes in history than could possibly have been known to anyone in former times. We have all—even now—experienced the joy and pain of such changes in the Church, which today occur unavoidably at a greater speed than formerly, simply because secular history also runs its course very much more rapidly.

Such unavoidable changes occurring more rapidly than formerly should not make us feel insecure, should not lead to indignation and protests, as if the old, to which we were accustomed, had always been better. If then it is asked what changes may be expected in the immediate future, over and above those experienced in recent decades, we may be a little embarrassed, if we are not clairvoyants or prophets. There is however something we can say. In a secularized world, in which nothing Christian can anywhere be simply taken for granted, the Church must be sustained even in its institutions and in its ministry much more than it is now by a readiness to believe freely on the part of its members at the base, on the part of basic communities; the latter will not be content simply to be cared for by an institutional Church, but will themselves on their own responsibility take an active part in forming the Church and will have a right to be taken seriously in their activity and responsibility by the authorities. At the same time, not a few things which are taken for granted in our own country as distinct from many other Churches in other countries will not continue to be so regarded, but will either disappear or demand for their maintenance a new and resolute sociopolitical commitment and also readiness for sacrifice on the part of Catholics. In many details of the symbiosis of the politically organized society and the Church—for example, with reference to the church-tax, religious instruction in state schools, theological faculties in state universities, state assistance for the Church's social institutions, the special sociological status of the Church, etc.—we cannot assume that everything in the future will go on as hitherto, peacefully and without question.

As far as the Church as a whole is concerned, it will turn to an increasing extent and increasingly rapidly from a European church with Christian exports to all the world into a world-Church, in which the churches of Africa, South America and even Asia, will be really autonomous elements with their own specific character and their own importance in the whole Church, justifying independently their existence and mission. We have already seen that, geographically speaking, Europe and Rome are by no means any longer at the centre of the Church. Such a world-Church as it exists outside Europe cannot simply import and imitate the life-style, law, liturgy and theology of the European church. In all these respects the churches outside Europe must be really independent and culturally firmly rooted in their own countries and—while maintaining the unity of faith and the link with the Pope—develop a new life of their own which we simply cannot imagine today and which at first sight might seem as alien to us as if we were attending today a Mass in the Syro-Malabar rite in South India. Of course, such a future prospect of the differentiation of the world-Church assumes that, despite the rational-technical world-civilization, the diversity of national and continental cultures will be maintained and even acquire a new vitality. In this world-Church, according to our Catholic faith, there will always be a Petrine ministry with its permanent and perhaps in some respects increasingly important tasks. Nevertheless, in the concrete way in which this ministry is exercised, a great deal will be changed, can be changed and must be changed.

It might perhaps be said briefly that the Pope for many centuries exercised his Petrine ministry to the whole Church in the style of a Patriarch of the West, that he tried to spread over the whole world the Latin Church of the West. Now however the churches that began as exports from Europe have become independent and force us clearly to distinguish between the dogmatically assured, authentic Petrine ministry to the whole Church and the Pope's function as Patriarch of the West, which remains a respectable but less important part of the Church as a whole and which in its concrete shape will no longer be oriented from Rome towards the whole Church. The Second Vatican Council marks a fresh start in the dialogue of Christianity and especially the Catholic Church with the present historical situation. But the beginning of this dialogue is not its end. From the very outset, correctly understood, this dialogue does not mean a faint-hearted compromise with any sort of spirit of the age. It can and must take place in the form of a critical and absolute opposition to a godless and greedy consumer mentality, largely drained of all authentic human feeling. It remains true however that the dialogue between the Church and the world must continue and that it demands also from the Church changes in its life-style, in the style of proclamation of the Christian faith, in the treatment of people who have come of age, in respect for freedom of conscience, in making apparent the workings of its official machinery, etc.

These changes in the Church as a whole necessarily have consequences for the church of our immediate neighbourhood, the church of our own country, of our homeland. As a result of the Council itself we have experienced such consequences in the last decade and we shall experience similar changes in the future. If we regard them as inevitable consequences of changes in the Church as a whole, they will seem less surprising and less depressing. Of course the opposite is also true. The changes arising in our own immediate neighbourhood, in our own country and in Europe, because of the shortage of priests, changes in the mental climate, changes in the concrete relations between Church and state, etc., will also have consequences for the Church as a whole.

In this unavoidably changing Church however something will endure. And this is also the unwavering answer of Christian faith to the question about the future of the Church. When we say that the Church will remain in the future, since its real message cannot perish, we are not merely setting out a prognosis of permanence on the grounds that there are constants even in history in the light of the true and lasting nature of man, but our prognosis of the future is based on the real message of Christianity itself, rightly understood. This message is not subject to time and time's changes, since it is itself the proclamation of the end of all time, since in the last resort and properly speaking it does not say that something remains of what we have now, that we are not deprived of our possessions: what it does say is that the absolute future—which is the eternal God himself, beyond all limits of time—will reach us as the fulfilment of time and history, whether the course of the changing times is long or short, whether it is filled with victories or with defeats. Since Christianity proclaims this end of history as the victory of God, its message can never be superseded by the announcement of something that always remains part of history as an interim goal. Within the course of time and a history that remains open, there may be much still to come, to be hoped for or feared, to be done or suffered: much that is always new, of which as yet we know nothing. But whatever is to come in the present world, however much and however surprising, is already encompassed by the message of Christianity which tells, not of this or that, but of all in one, of God as beginning and end and as such as our own consummation. This message—not only issued in words, but present and sealed in the event of Jesus Christ, who died into the incomprehensibility of God and was thus vindicated—can never again be lost to humanity as a whole. For it is the supreme and unsurpassable hope, nourished by humanity's victories *and* defeats, since the brief moments of light in history and the times of great darkness alike bear witness to the eternal light, the light announced in Jesus Christ as forever victorious.

How could the message of Christianity be superseded, when it proclaims, not just one thing or another, but the pure infinity of God as the absolute future of humanity? How could this message be unmasked as an unreal Utopia when it arises from the very event which unmasks all illusions, from death itself, from the death of Jesus, in face of which humanity did not despair but learned to hope absolutely? The message of Christianity for a future does not proclaim the replacement of what exists here and now by something else that is likewise under the law of coming to be and perishing, but the salvation of all by that infinite, incomprehensible reality, exalted above all coming to be and perishing, which we call God. If this message does not perish and cannot perish, since it is the answer to humanity's infinite hope, then neither does the Church perish, being the fellowship of those who in faith and hope make this message the centre of their existence.

As we pointed out at the beginning, this message and the community of those who carry it are ultimately independent of the proportion between the number of these believers and the total number of human beings. The message is the promise for mankind as a whole, even though it is expressly supported only by a few. It is a message that has in fact been implicitly accepted and taken to heart by those who hope absolutely, even though they do not venture to express the immensity of their hopes in words and phrases. But, if this infinite message of Christianity is brought quite clearly to an individual and in a way that demands his faith, it is not for him alone as an individual to decide whether he will accept it or not. If the message reaches him in this way, he must take his place in the company of those who form the Church and thus proclaim the message to the world and keep it alive in the world's history. That is the way in which the message was brought to us; it reached us in such a way that we must be its heralds and not merely its recipients and hearers. The Christian and the communities of Christians, as present or as represented here, are the Church which has to bear the burden of its own past, which must face its present with the courage to profess Christianity in word and life, with courage for the changes required by the existing situation, in loyalty in faith to the Christian message and in unshakeable hope for the future of the Church, since it is the profession of eternal hope which will not perish.

The future of the Church of our European nations can be predicted only with difficulty or not at all. It is the object, not of futurological calculation, but of each individual's eternal responsibility; and it grows, not out of futurology, but out of the unconditional loyalty of faith on the part of each individual. But we know that, if the European nations, if we, let fall the torch of faith, hope and love, then other peoples will carry it through history to its end. The future of the Church is God and consequently eternal life for us.

9

STRUCTURAL CHANGE IN THE CHURCH
OF THE FUTURE

T HE THEME presented to the author here is so broad and
complex that only a few remarks of an aphoristic character are
possible within the space at his disposal; the reader then cannot
expect a really systematic and comprehensive treatment. These limitations arise also from the fact that the author is not a church historian,
nor a futurologist, nor a canonist, and consequently cannot claim any
special competence in these fields of study which as such are relevant to
the subject. He is merely a systematic, dogmatic theologian, for whom
what is important and must be important is the permanent and perennially valid element of ecclesiology in the light of revelation. For the
dogmatic theologian therefore the essential question is that of the possibilities of a structural change of the Church in a future secular society,
in the light of the Catholic Church's existing and permanent self-understanding based on revelation. But, even if the question is raised in this
way from the outset, the author is sure that such opportunities for
structural change in the Church are extraordinarily great, although they
are often not seen clearly enough even as mere opportunities and the
institutional Church here in Germany and also in Rome (the author
would not claim to be able to say anything significant about other regional churches, which are parts of the one Church) looks too hesitatingly
and too nervously at these possible changes of the Church's structures.[1]

Leaving aside any subtle politological and juridical definitions of
terms, by 'structures' here is meant simply everything that exists in fact

---

[1] Cf. Karl Rahner, *Strukturwandel der Kirche als Aufgabe und Chance* (Freiburg 1972);
ET: *The Shape of the Church to Come* (London/New York 1974).

in the Church (as a whole or in a regional church) permanently and universally as a reality determining the action and decisions of the office-holders and church-members or as a norm for this action and these decisions. In this respect it is in the last resort a matter of indifference whether these determinants of action are simply factual conditions or legally constituted norms, whether they affect that action as the result of an explicit, considered decision or simply exercise their influence in practice, whether in themselves they are really ecclesial in character or (in the light of the Church's theological understanding of its nature) purely secular, as factors belonging to secular society.

I

During the 'Pian epoch' of the Church (if we may so describe the period of restoration in society and the Church after the French Revolution of 1789 up to the Second Vatican Council), in the Church's self-under-standing the stress was laid on its 'unchangeability'. The Church was regarded as the stronghold and sign of what was eternally valid in an increasingly rapidly changing course of history, moving towards an indeterminate future in which nothing would any longer be secure and permanent. The Church insisted on its constitution *jure divino* as unchangeable, given to it from the outset by God himself in Jesus Christ (at the same time the fact that this knowledge of its divine foundation became explicit only in the course of history had little effect in practice on the Church's actual self-awareness). The Church insisted that its papal and episcopal constitutional structure was of divine law, coming from 'above', from Jesus Christ, and had not been set up 'democratically' from below. The First Vatican Council sanctioned as part of the immutable content of faith and of the Church's divinely established constitutional structure the Bishop of Rome's universal primacy of jurisdiction and supreme teaching authority—independently of the consent of the Church—over the Church as a whole and over all its particular churches.

There was a similar insistence during this period on an immutable natural law, from which concrete conclusions were drawn in regard to the most diverse fields of men's moral and social life. At least tacitly and in practice the impression prevailed that the institutional Church's life and action, even in their concrete expression, by and large, were the quite straightforward and immediately obvious, indisputable consequences of the Church's perennially valid constitutional law and of the natural law: the institutional Church's concrete action was regarded as the almost self-evident manifestation of what is permanently valid in the Church.

Even during this Pian epoch there were of course some not inconsiderable changes in the structures (in the sense explained above) of the Church. With the secularized states concordats of various kinds were concluded, also with important consequences for the internal life of the Church. The liturgy continued to develop towards the far-reaching changes at the Second Vatican Council. There were quite significant changes in the Church's marriage laws. The college of cardinals as an elective body was slowly internationalized. If, on the whole, the 'new' Canon Law under Benedict XV was no more than an adjustment of the Church's existing law and practice, it really was 'new' in some respects and brought about a degree of change in the Church. In addition to these and similar changes in the structures of the Church at this time, there were certainly many others that could be mentioned. But on the whole the stress and the feeling of the self-understanding of the Church were concentrated during this period on unchangeability. And even for those who were aware of the great and lively history of the dogma and constitution of the Church in this self-understanding from the primitive Church to the Pian epoch, the impression prevailed that the Church had reached in its development a point from which there could be no return and beyond which not much really new or surprising was likely to happen. All this was worked out in terms of neoscholastic theology.

There were certainly two reasons why the stress (itself historically conditioned and changeable) in this self-understanding of the Church was laid on its 'unchangeability'. On the one hand, in face of a world which had been increasingly rapidly secularized from the time of the Enlightenment onwards, the Church was bound to feel threatened and had to find its means of existence in itself and no longer in a homogeneous Christian society; the forms of the intellectual life of secular society seemed alien to its own traditional shape; from the time of the Enlightenment also, it felt itself increasingly confronted by a militant anticlericalism. Not surprisingly in this situation, the Church became much more clearly aware of its own nature as distinct from the world and unchangeable. The other reason, closely linked with the first, lay in the fact that medieval and baroque theology (as preserved and revived in neoscholasticism) was and remains oriented *a priori* more or less unhistorically to the eternal essences of things, to what is permanently valid, and did not and does not sufficiently allow for the fact that history itself is precisely the history of essences and of man's transcendence to God, not merely the sphere of the contingent, surrounded externally by the realm of eternal essences. In brief, during this epoch culminating in the First Vatican Council, the stress of the Church's self-understanding lay on its unchangeability, on the permanent validity of its nature and those constitutional structures which must be seriously taken into account, as well as elements admittedly changeable in themselves but regarded as participating to a certain extent in this permanent validity. (In a scholastic Denzinger-theology, for example, authentic statements of the magisterium were treated in practice as if they had the binding force of dogma and measures passed by curial officials regarded almost as straightforward decisions of the Pope using his supreme power of jurisdiction.)

There is no doubt that the feeling has grown and become more distinct since the Second Vatican Council that the Church is changeable in all its structures to a far greater extent than people thought during the Pian epoch. The reasons for this change in the Church's concrete self-understanding will not be set out here, particularly since they are obviously many and varied. In exegesis and history of dogma, theology has gradually roused an awareness generally in the Church of the historicity even of dogma and of the dogmatically formulated structures of the Church. It has now become clearer, and the view was sanctioned to a certain extent by Vatican II (despite reactionary trends after the Council in recent years), that the Church, now become a world-Church, must live in a secularized and pluralistic world and yet be engaged in missionary activity and present in quite new cultural fields beyond that of an older Europe; that it cannot simply live on the defensive, in a traditional and merely reactionary way; that—while remaining faithful to its message and to its own nature arising from that message—it needs an *aggiornamento,* an adaptation, to the world in which it must live and grow; that it must become involved in new, unforeseen situations, not brought about by itself but by which it is itself necessarily changed, since today in the age of scientific planning and futurology such changes (which have always existed) cannot take place tacitly and unobtrusively, without premeditation, but must also be considered and planned in advance. But—as we said—we are not going to consider here the reasons for this change of feeling and its necessity. All that can be done is to point to a number of somewhat arbitrarily chosen and unsystematically presented particular examples that show, even to the Catholic who completely accepts the defined dogma of the nature of the Church, that the possibilities of such structural changes in the Church are much greater than they were thought to be in the Pian epoch. Whether the realization of particular individual possibilities is opportune or appropriate to the present and future external situation of the Church is another question.

First of all we have the Roman See, the task and function of the Pope, as these were defined by Vatican I and acknowledged as continuing to be valid by Vatican II. It is becoming increasingly clear and more apparent in the Church's self-understanding that this supreme and permanent power of jurisdiction of the Pope for the whole Church is not simply identical with the whole gigantic administrative machinery which has developed historically and continues to exist and operate up to the present time in Rome. The demarcation between what the Pope admits and up to a point must admit to belong to the autonomous competence of the particular churches and what he reserves to himself for the most part is not a matter of divine law, but has come to existence historically and is therefore changeable. For it cannot be claimed that the concrete and changeable settlement of this demarcation is simply dependent on a decision of the Pope, not rationally to be justified and not open to appeal, solely because the Pope is not subject to any higher earthly decision-making authority in the Church to which an appeal might legally be made. This demarcation, which is constantly in need of revision, can certainly be decided by objective arguments, even if the latter also take into account the Pope's understanding of the issue; with reference to the relationship between the universal government of the whole Church in Rome and the individual particular churches and their life, all general norms of Christian morality and of a system of law understood in a truly Christian sense (norms for exceptional cases, *epikeia,* tacit excuse, etc.) are genuinely valid and should be applied without hesitation.

The creation of concrete individual norms, which are to be valid for the Church as a whole, should be brought about with an institutionalized and obvious collaboration of the regional churches. In the light of the Church's constitution as based on divine law, all this is certainly feasible and could be urgently necessary to prevent wrong decisions or norms imposing too many restrictions on individual particular churches; but in practice this collaboration has not yet been institutionalized and made obvious to a sufficiently large extent and where progress has been made it has been dependent on the good will of the Roman authorities in regard to a particular case. The internationalization of the Roman Curia has certainly made considerable progress since Vatican II, but it has not come about with the obvious collaboration of the authorities of the particular churches, the result being that the Curia has been internationalized more or less only in regard to the birthplace of its members: the latter cannot really be regarded as representatives of the churches from which they come, although this is really supposed to be the point of internationalization. (This is not to say that these internationally qualified curial officials ought to be representatives of their countries of origin in a strictly legal sense. But, on the other hand, it is noticeable that members of the Curia become quickly 'romanized', lose any real contacts with their countries of origin and become more Roman than the Romans.)

If what follows has a wider reference than merely to the relationship between Rome and the particular churches, it should be observed in the present context that it is quite compatible with the Pope's universal jurisdiction defined at Vatican I as in a certain sense 'unlimited' (and thus allowing for possibilities of changing the concrete structures of the Church) that this primatial power of the Pope is also restricted and by human law can impose on itself limits required by a particular historical situation. It is limited in the first place (apart from the limits imposed by Christian morality, which even the Pope may infringe under certain circumstances by a concrete act in such a way that the latter not only offends morality, but perhaps also is legally invalid) by divine law, in so far as the Pope—according to the teaching of Vatican II—cannot abolish the episcopate, cannot replace it by office-holders who would be merely his officials; in so far also as the individual bishop governs his church, not only in the name of the Pope, but immediately in the name of Christ himself. This principle of Vatican II sounds innocuous, particularly since, according to current legislation (which of course is not unchangeable, even though the individual bishop, if he wants to govern legitimately, must live in unity and peace with the Roman See), the Pope appoints the individual bishop. But this principle, if taken seriously and given concrete expression, could also have far-reaching effects on the concrete structures of the Church. For it means that an individual bishop is not merely a regional executive official of Rome, carrying out on the spot what is decreed by Rome for the whole Church.On the contrary, he can take spiritual and administrative initiatives; these need not be seen from the very outset and always purely as applications of Roman norms and authorized for that reason; in teaching also (for example, in concrete questions of morality) the bishop as such has his own initiative from the spirit of the gospel and need not always—for example, in concrete questions of Christian morality and of real life—be positively supported by Roman approval, merely because these questions have their importance everywhere in the Church. We might get the impression that our own bishops do not sufficiently appreciate the scope which this principle accords them or the possibilities of structural change it implies, that they act too frequently as if they were merely carrying out orders from Rome and wanting in every case to be positively 'covered' from there.

There are however limits to the Roman primatial power which that authority itself can and under certain circumstances must lay down in human law and which in the concrete involve changes in the actual historical form of papal constitutional law. In the first place no one will dispute the fact that the Holy See has made and can legitimately make concordats with states. And in such concordats (however they are to be interpreted in the light of the different theories on the subject), not infrequently, the Roman See restricts by a legal agreement the rights and the authority belonging to it 'as such'. For example, it may concede to a state a considerable degree of collaboration in the selection of candidates for the episcopate, it may grant to other authorities *jure humano* real and permanent rights that belong as such *jure divino* to itself alone. If this sort of thing is possible in relations between Church and state, it can be possible also in relations between the Roman See and other authorities and groups within the Church. There are in fact situations in which it would be not only possible, but also opportune and even morally necessary. Rights in regard to the appointment of bishops, to the organization of the liturgy, to sacramental practice, the laws of marriage, etc., which the Holy See claims in virtue of its authority *jure divino,* can be restricted by itself in favour of the particular churches and their independent existence appropriate to their own situation. (At the same time the original claim to these rights need not be simply unambiguous, even though for the sake of unity and peace in the Church the Pope must be granted the competence to decide his own competence and consequently not all Canon Law in the concrete is simply deduced from first principles, nor can it be established by a strictly rational argument.) Consequently, something of this kind can be wholly opportune and even concretely necessary.

It is not as if the appointment of bishops, the norms for selecting priests (e.g., the law of celibacy, exclusion of women from the priesthood, definition of the grades of the sacramental ministry), etc., had *necessarily* to be laid down by Rome for the whole Church. In these and similar matters Rome could leave a great deal to the particular churches and should not from the very outset invoke the Pope's universal power of jurisdiction or the necessary unity of the Church in order to block such possibilities (it is not a question of more than this). Greater rights could be conceded to the particular churches, even if this concession meant or could at least be interpreted as an act of the supreme authority in the Church. (Not that every such concession necessarily has to be interpreted as a free act of favour on the part of Rome. Even Rome will not claim that the greater autonomy of the Eastern Uniate Churches—which it recognizes—is due simply to a free act of favour on the part of Rome which it could withdraw without more ado. The attitude which Rome adopts towards these autonomies of the Eastern Church, arising from the past, could also become at least a moral obligation in regard to autonomies of the particular churches to be acknowledged by Rome in view of the requirements of the future.) In brief, the right (which can also be a duty) of the supreme universal authority of Rome to decide its own limits in the Church permits in principle considerable flexibility in the concrete expression of this *jus divinum:* despite and even in its permanent validity, the latter is a historical factor open to change and continually permitting new forms of expression of its own nature and practice, even though these cannot directly be foreseen and will depend on future historical conditions. The great centralistic machinery of Rome, the multiplicity and allocation of offices, the range of tasks which Rome reserves to itself, the form of papal elections, the universal Canon Law covering the smallest details, the frequency of Rome's reactions to particular questions arising in all parts of the world, etc., are certainly not matters of divine law; they are changeable and always open to the critical question as to whether such concrete forms of the exercise of the universal papal authority are really appropriate to the concrete historical situation. (For the moment, it may be noticed incidentally that this is a question of great ecumenical importance.)

As far as the possibilities of structural change in the greater regional, particular churches are concerned, the question today is concretely that of the possibility and opportuneness of fitting 'more democratic' structures into these individual churches (dioceses, national churches). What is important in this connection is certainly not the term 'democracy'; it is obvious that these churches neither can nor should simply copy the decision-making 'democratic' structures in the secular field in their own countries, but they must take into account realistically the problems of 'democracy' even in that field (we need only recall, apart from other things, the threat to such 'democracy' from 'democratic centralism' in what are known as the 'socialist' countries). What is important in the concrete is the necessity (particularly today and always involved in the very nature of the Church) for the collaboration of churchpeople in the life of the Church and the decisions of authority. In the light of the Church's nature churchpeople are not merely recipients of what is done by the institutional Church but are themselves the Church. And today (later we must speak of this at greater length) the real efficacy of the Church's ministries (proclamation, administration of the sacraments, government, etc.) depends largely on the free collaboration of churchgoers themselves. This however is not to be expected, unless the people are obviously involved to the greatest possible extent in the decision-making of the institutional Church. Nor is this necessary participation to be expected in practice if it is to be merely informal; it needs juridical and visible structures which themselves are not in every case necessarily dependent on the good will of the office-holders strictly so called.

The duties of such collaboration by the churchpeople, stressed as they are on all sides, can be concretely fulfilled only if they correspond to real and perceptible rights. Certainly, since the Second Vatican Council, people have been engaged everywhere in creating such new juridically constituted structures for the collaboration of churchgoers in the Church's life and decision-making, beginning perhaps with parish councils. Nor should the fact be overlooked that, by the very nature of the Church, this collaboration and the legal structures on which it depends can and must take very different forms in the light of the concrete issues to be settled. (Collaboration in regard to the Church's finances can and must certainly take a different form from that of organizing the innermost centre of the liturgy or dealing with a question relating to the faith of the Church as a whole.) The particular opportunities for such new structures of the collaboration of the churchpeople in the Church's life and decision-making cannot of course be considered here.

All that we can do is to point to a fundamental principle that can be put into effect without more ado in the formation of such new structures. In principle even the *jure divino* episcopal constitution of the Church does not mean that the collaboration of churchgoers can and must always and in every case be merely informative and advisory, merely of a consultative character. If in the early Church the people and the ordinary clergy had the right to an essential part in the deliberations leading to the appointment of a new bishop, this was certainly not an infringement of the perennially valid episcopal constitution any more than the proprietary Church *(Eigenkirche)* of the early Middle Ages (where ecclesiastical appointments were under the control of the secular ruler), even though such juridical conditions cannot be copied without more ado for present or future times. Certainly there are matters to be decided even today and in the future in which the collaboration of the people, not only in a consultative but also in a deliberative form, would be possible and appropriate.

There are certainly many issues where the churchpeople could and even should share in decision-making and in which the individual bishop or a bishops' conference could not be bound by the decision only if that authority could declare conscientiously that it was clearly contrary to the substance of the Church's faith or to the *jure divino* constitution of the Church: that is, in a situation analogous to that of a state where the supreme constitutional court (like the episcopate in the Church) declares that a law passed by Parliament is unconstitutional. In no other case should the episcopate (or an individual bishop in his own diocese) invoke episcopal authority in a decision contrary to the will of the majority of the people, if only because such decisions today are likely to remain ineffective in practice. That in fact was the situation at the Würzburg Synod in 1971, when in not a few cases—even those in which no conscientious reservation could be made—the German bishops actually decided in a way contrary to that of the existing or foreseeable majority of the people attending there. This sort of thing is not necessary in virtue of the Church's constitutional law and not appropriate today, since it creates the impression that the bishops eventually decide solely according to their own discretion (even after listening to the representatives of the laity and the clergy) and in questions in which it is not at all necessary to reserve such a competence to themselves.

If the principle of a possible deliberative and not merely consultative collaboration of the people in the decisions of the institutional Church were seen more clearly and institutionalized more courageously, this would do something to rouse the laity from mere acquiescence and indifference. And in particular, regional churches the opportunities of structural change in the Church are still far from being exhausted, even though there remain very many unanswered questions as to how this sort of thing could and should be brought about in an appropriate way and in the light of a realistic appraisal of the concrete situation.

II

The full title of this chapter is: 'Structural change of the Church in the *future* society'.

To be honest, it must be admitted that what has been said up to now—properly speaking—does not really even touch on this theme or at best touches on it only remotely. For all that has hitherto been said, and in a very abstract way, is that structural change is *possible* in the Church, despite the latter's enduring nature. What possible changes of the Church's structures are opportune and desirable for the Church's endurance and life cannot be settled merely by such theoretical reflections. In order to answer the question which was really supposed to be the theme of these reflections, we would have to know what is likely to be the shape of the secular society in which the Church will have to live and in which it must develop its concrete structures in dialogue and confrontation, in order to secure as well as possible its endurance, its life and its missionary activity in that future society.

But what will this future society look like? Can anyone say? It is possible to maintain—and, up to a point, rightly—that the present structures of the Church are not sufficiently adapted even to society *today* and that in this respect also there is still a good deal of leeway to be made up. It can be said that much in the present-day structures of the Church has not yet been brought into line adequately (naturally, with the aid of dialogue) with the conditions of a secularized and pluralistic society; that the Church in many respects relies too much on sociological conditions (what remains of the symbiosis of state, society and Church, peculiarities of a rural or middle-class society, relics of Christian values even in the secularized society, etc.) which still exist up to a point, but meet with increasing resistance and are now being rapidly eliminated. Certainly it can also be said that even today the actual effectiveness of the institutional Church in regard to individuals is no longer backed by a consensus on a Christian weltanschauung that is taken for granted in civic society, but needs to be sustained by living basic communities built up from below, formed by a free decision of faith on the part of individuals *against* public trends in society; that the institutional structures of the Church no longer sustain the faith of individuals as in former times, but (so far as their actual efficacy is concerned) are themselves sustained by this faith.

In face of this simple observation of the Church's present situation, it is certainly possible to set up very diverse postulates for a change in the Church's structures, while upholding the permanence of its ultimate nature: for a greater 'democratization' (rightly understood) of the Church, not restricting the collaborations of the 'laity' to purely consultative functions but giving it a form appropriate to each particular issue; for greater openness in decision-making in the Church's life, even for the non-clerical members of the Church; for greater autonomy of the major, particular, regional churches within the one Church; for the opportuneness or necessity today of those things which we have already suggested as possible in principle in the light of the Church's nature. If we could bring them under the heading of structural change in the widest sense of the term, it would be possible in such reflections even today to speak of a declericalized, serving, caring Church, preaching morality without moralizing, being open to secular society, boldly giving concrete directives for public life without always declaring these to be permanently valid dogma or part of the unchanging content of natural law, socially critical without seeking to dictate to secular society or restrict its autonomy. But we shall not go into further detail here about these postulates of structural change perceptible from the very situation of present-day society, however much reflections of this kind in terms of practical (and political) theology are still required today.

In speaking about these things however, have we or could we have really said anything about structural change of the Church in the society of the *future?* Is it possible at the present time to say anything *about this* or can we speak about it only when the future society actually exists? Or are we to say, we must talk about it now, since the Church must approach its future looking forward to it and equipped for it? Or are we to say that it is impossible to talk about it yet, since secular futurology predicts much about the world of the future but says scarcely anything that is at present obviously relevant to a structural change by which the *Church* can and must be prepared for a future society? What special features of a future epoch could perhaps be foreseen which might be important for a structural change in the Church to be prepared even now? (For example, is it not even now time to begin a theological reflection about whether the seat of the primacy in the Church will have to remain in Rome in the future, when the real centres of power and authority will no longer lie in the older Europe?) These are hard questions. The Church must always be aware of the fact that questions like this are not irrelevant and are not to be suppressed merely because there is no obvious answer to them, acceptable to all sides. For even open, unsolved questions—if they are not suppressed—keep alive the willingness to bring about such structural changes promptly when they become necessary: they have then a very concrete significance.

For the time being however, one thing at least can be said. In a future society, in a secularized world, all the elements of which are everywhere interdependent, Christendom will be able adequately to fulfil its function as sacrament of the salvation of the world only by itself becoming more of a unity than it has been hitherto. Everything that is sought by the ecumenical movement is also a task imposed on Christendom by and for a future society. But this also necessarily means that the Catholic Church even now must boldly set to work on all those structural changes which on the one hand are possible in the light of its nature and on the other hand can help the separated Christian Churches more easily to appreciate their solidarity and more easily to unite with one another until a real unity of the one Church of Christ is reached. Ecumenism is a task which is certainly imposed also by a future society and must carry with it considerable structural changes in the Catholic Church, particularly since in the future even more than now this Catholic Church cannot remain the Church of the West, sending small exports to the rest of the world, but must really be a world-Church where the different cultures and spheres of history enjoy equal rights.

When ecumenism is becoming an urgent task of the Catholic Church, acquiring quite new dimensions, because of the future society, must not the great, particular churches (for example, in Africa, Asia and Latin America) be granted quite new fields for the actualizations of their own natures? Can those theological questions which once divided the churches in the world of the Mediterranean and of Europe retain their importance in the world of today? Can the law of the world-Church remain as 'Roman' as it was formerly? Must not the question of mutual recognition of ministries be tackled with much more theological energy and confidence, while aiming at a generous (and possible) solution, than it has been hitherto when there was too much fear and (if we may so express it) too little theological imagination? When this sort of thing and so much else is appreciated and its realization facilitated, does it not necessitate in the Catholic Church very considerable structural changes, which must be seen to be possible and must be prepared for the sake of the future society, so that as far as possible a *united* Christendom can exist and fulfil its task in this future society?

It is very difficult and may well be impossible to predict anything about the future situation of the Church (as starting point for postulates of structural change), since it is difficult to foresee anything about the future society that is also relevant to the Church. When we say that the life of the future society will be that of a rational and technical world-civilization, in which all the formerly separate cultural and historical fields will be intensely concentrated, in an urban culture, in a society which will have developed higher sociological structures than existed or were necessary formerly, we are saying something which is true on the whole but from which anything about a necessary structural change in the Church can be deduced only with difficulty. One thing however should be clear: nowhere in the world will the Church of the future live in a society homogeneously Christian by nature and, as a secular society, taking for granted and supporting the Church's activity. That much can be said, even if the question remains open as to what economic systems (themselves understood as ideologically binding) will prevail or be alone dominant in this one world-civilization. Everywhere in the world the Church will be a Diaspora-Church, no longer existing within the homogeneous ambience of a Christian Europe, even though the numerical relationship between Christians (who are actually such) and non-Christians (who never were Christians or who have again become non-Christians) may remain very different in the different individual cultural and sociological areas of the one world-civilization.

If the Church in a future society will everywhere be a Diaspora-Church, its mission and message in the world will no longer be favoured and supported from the very outset by a homogeneous public opinion, by laws it has itself inspired, by a general acceptance of the position of its leaders. The Church will be an individual sociological group in a pluralist society and then only if the rest of society is tolerantly pluralistic in a liberal sense—something also which cannot be predicted with certainty. Consequently the real effectiveness of such a Church and of its authorities will depend—and in fact much more decisively than in Europe in the past—on the assent of faith freely given by individuals and the commitment of its members 'from below'. What has hitherto been regarded more or less as an 'established' Church will become a community-Church; parishes (as administrative districts set up by ecclesiastical authority and evenly spread over a certain territory) will have to become living communities from below, not from the outset directly bordering territorially on one another, sharing much more clearly than formerly in the determination of their ecclesial life-style, in the selection of their 'officials', and deciding the mode of life of the latter (allowing always for the permanent necessity of common ecclesial structures and the unity— maintained by bishops—of the individual congregations with one another), maintaining unity of faith with a diversity of emphasis on the various aspects of their Christian and ecclesial life, etc.

The community Church is not in opposition to the Church as made up of territorial parishes, even though the latter as locally constituted will exist in future alongside personally constituted parishes with a different basis, in greater numbers and having greater significance. Parishes in the traditional sense will themselves have to become living community parishes more clearly than hitherto and can no longer remain (more or less) institutions by which the official Church provides for the individual religious needs of isolated individuals.

In the light of this Diaspora situation of the future Church, then, considerable structural changes in the Church must be expected and are clearly beginning to take shape even now, although in our own country we might get the impression that the institutional Church is giving way to pressure in regard to these changes or merely tolerating them, not anticipating or leading. The future Church consisting of communities in Diaspora situations will of course always be in danger of becoming a 'sect' in a negative sense in terms of the sociology of religion. This danger of becoming a 'little flock' in the wrong sense of the term, with an élitist self-consciousness and an ideologically justified incapsulation of the community and its members from the general cultural and sociological life to windward of history, must be recognized and opposed. Difficult as this may be in detail, the structures of the future community-churches must be shaped so as to face as squarely as possible the danger that the community might become the refuge of people whom life has treated badly, who have suffered at the hands of society and its members; the community must be open to all and aware of its continuing function toward the 'world'. If we thus anticipate future and necessary structural changes on a large scale in the Church, if a timid conservatism does not blind us to the necessity and depth of these future changes, although of course the continuity beneath the change from today to tomorrow cannot be denied, then there emerges as a postulate of the Church's strategy what has been called a tutiorism of change.

What is required now is not timid conservatism, uncreatively yielding when it seems that nothing more can be done, least of all at the present time. In the long run, the safest course and the one that will do least harm is to muster the courage now to attempt what in all probability will be demanded of the institutional Church tomorrow. Why is it so timid and hesitant about the question of the rights that can be granted to lay-people in the Church without detriment to its papal and episcopal structure, even though it knows that tomorrow it will presumably have as members only those who acknowledge it as a result of a deeply felt Christian decision and not as liberal-minded traditional Christians? Why are people so fearful and concerned about a Roman centralism that is always in danger of imposing an undue uniformity on the living structures and forces in individual major particular churches, thus rendering the latter ineffective? Why does not Rome have the courage to attempt a *new* language in declarations and decisions which might then have some prospect of 'getting across' to the world? These and many other similar questions could be raised. A mentality regarding risk and experiment—the outcome of which is not yet certain—perhaps as the safest and necessary course for today and tomorrow, without immediately holding back in fear of disorder and diverging trends in the particular churches, certainly could and should creatively and courageously inaugurate many structural changes in the Church.

III

As in every society, so too in the Church, there will always be conservative *and* progressive trends, both of which in principle are necessary and useful when change must be combined with continuity. If then we are talking about structural change in the Church and if our endeavours are to find concrete expression, there will always be people, including office-holders, in the Church who are for and against these changes, particularly since the latter cannot simply be deduced from the very nature of the Church or from an analysis of the situation at the time—an analysis which can never be really complete—but remain matters of discretion, so that the antagonism between conservative and progressive forces in the Church can never be wholly eliminated. It might even be said that, despite the enduring unity of the Church and the love that must prevail in it, this antagonism in some respects is more acute than it is in any other, secular society. It is really easy to see the reason for this and the clear awareness of the reason could help to a certain extent to defuse the antagonism. In secular societies decisions for or against structural change (unless they are radically revolutionary decisions in face of radically revolutionary situations) are mostly matters of discretion and refer to objects which can easily be seen to be of merely relative importance.

Within the Church also structural changes as such are concerned with similarly relative realities which are part of the present world and the sphere of the human. But churchgoing believers regard these things (rightly, in principle) as related in some sense 'sacramentally' to the properly divine sphere, to man's eternal destiny and salvation. That is why, despite their essential relativity, these things have a significance and importance for the believer going substantially beyond that of purely secular realities. These things (the word of Scripture, the properly sacramental signs and a great deal more of what is involved in the concrete structures of the Church) secure the relationship of the believer to the eternal. If he then gets the impression that these familiar realities in the Church establish authentically and vitally his relationship to God and his salvation or if he begins to feel that they are making this relationship difficult or even obstructing it, he will be inclined to apply himself with a passion for the eternal to defend the permanence of these realities or to insist on changing them. That is why dogmatic conflicts, even though they appear at first sight to be merely about 'forms', are carried on so passionately and stubbornly in the Church; that is why wars of religion have been carried on so relentlessly; that is why, over and over again in the Church, there have been passionate and stubborn conflicts about what might seem to outsiders or to those living at a later time to be almost ludicrously unimportant (from the date of Easter in the early Church to the modern reform of the Mass liturgy).

The struggle about earthly things in the Church is often carried on with a passion usually devoted to the eternal, since the two cannot very easily be clearly distinguished either objectively or emotionally. But if the distinction is seen and made clear in regard to the controversies on true or false structural changes in the Church it could help to defuse the struggles up to a point. The 'progressives' should not assume that their wishes are absolute (new proclamation of the gospel, new shaping of the liturgy, more 'democratic' structures of the internal life of the Church, better and bolder fulfilment of the Church's mission to the world, etc.). They must see that it is possible to work for salvation, to love God and neighbour, even in the 'old' Church; that in this Church too, despite all justified desires for reform, it is possible to be a Christian; that in the traditional Church also (even if it ought to be different and better and if we must work and struggle to make it so) there is nothing in principle to deny the Christian a true and radical Christianity, particularly since a critical approach to the traditional structures of the Church is itself not only a natural right of man but a Christian right and a specific task of the Christian as such in the Church as such. On the other hand, the 'conservatives' must learn that in individual cases they may well judge rightly on matters of discretion, but that what they want is likewise only of relative importance. (For instance, the controversy about Latin or the vernacular in the liturgy: both are of relative importance, both are purely matters of discretion, it is possible to pray in both languages, it is possible to fight for either side, everyone can and must accept in patience and the love of unity a decision which always remains provisional, on whatever lines it is made by one authority or another.) Conservatives *and* progressives can prematurely and by over-simplification associate or even identify what is relative and historically conditioned with what is eternal and perennially valid. Then the conflict between the opportuneness or inopportuneness of structural changes in the Church becomes radicalized and poisoned; then the necessary tolerance, with which such a conflict and the decisions in such a conflict must take place, no longer exists and the conflict becomes profoundly un-Christian, because—on one side or the other or even on both sides—God, his salvation and his grace, are identified with things that simply are not God, but are subject to the changes of history, which demands change in continuity and continuity through change.

10

DREAM OF THE CHURCH

I HAVE A dream to relate. This is difficult. For, as far as I can discover subsequently, I rarely dream. Moreover, this dream that I have to relate has to do with the Church. And in this respect it is easy to have nightmares. But this is to be a fine, hopeful dream. All of which creates further difficulties. Nor, on the whole, is the Church a particularly attractive object for a dream. But if I am to dream of something vividly concrete, being a Catholic theologian, what occurs to me almost inevitably is Rome with the Pope; and, since it is to be linked with the future, the dream must create hope for the future unity of Christendom. Since however a good dream should not be too fantastic, this dream was in fact as I shall relate it.

With a former student of mine I was going up one of the fine staircases in the Vatican. Oddly enough this student had been employed as a theologian in the Vatican itself. This was not something that might have been taken for granted. For my students are more likely to be regarded there with suspicion. But sometimes things turn out well. Perhaps the reason for this lucky chance was that it was spring 1985 when we were going up this staircase, although there had been lifts even in the Vatican for a long time.

'I am taking you with me', said the student, 'to one of the sessions which are taking place here at the present time, at which about a dozen of the leading representatives of the Christian Churches from all over the world come to meet the Pope for a friendly conversation about the possibility at last of the ecumenical movement going beyond non-committal expressions of friendship by church leaders and profound discus-

133

sions by theologians, after it has been stagnating for ten years. The churchmen sit at a round table, so that it is not obvious who is above and who is below. The Pope permits one or two theologians to listen to the debates, a little to one side, particularly since they were engaged in preparing the documents for these discussions. It is not the first session, everything has been going well for some time, supervision at the door is a mere formality; I can easily take you with me without being noticed.'

Soon the session started. The people really had come from all parts of the world. You could see it in their faces. The whites were very numerous, but no longer a majority. The actual participants at first stood around talking in a relaxed way, then the Pope also came. Mutual greetings took place without ceremony, as between old friends. An African Protestant clergyman said a prayer. I did not get the impression that this was a mere ritual, of the kind usual before official church business is transacted. The Pope gave an impression of frankness and cheerfulness, reminding me by his lack of solemn dignity agreeably of John XXIII. He spoke English. What else could he have done? What he said was more or less as follows.

THE POPE'S SUGGESTION

'Gentlemen, dear brothers! We have certainly made good progress in our common efforts, even though we are still involved in the first—the dogmatic—section of our discussions and have not yet got down at all to any of the canonical, liturgical, pastoral questions. Today we come to what is certainly the most difficult of these dogmatic questions—that of the papal primacy in the Church—and in this first part of our negotiations to the question of the papal *primacy of teaching*, as this is understood in the Roman Catholic Church. What I have to say on this question is explained at greater length in the papers you have already received and—I assume—submitted to a critical examination. Consequently I will only indicate briefly once again the decisive points of this written report.

First of all, this report assumes that the question before us cannot be solved by drawing a practical conclusion from exegetical and historical investigations, important as these may be. This is what the Churches have been trying to do for four hundred years, but without result. We must at last accept the consequences and try a different method. I think we should start out from those convictions in the Churches which are regarded in a given Church as essential to the Christian faith. With convictions of this kind, regarded as absolute (not that all opinions in the Churches are so regarded), it should be assumed in principle that they are true and consequently compatible with one another, although hitherto no one could or would see this compatibility. We should also start out from the assumption that in the Churches to be united not every proposition which one Church expressly affirms with an absolute commitment of faith is bound to have the same weight also in every other Church and must likewise be taught—even here and now—as an indisputable article of faith. All that needs to be assumed is that it is not absolutely rejected in this other Church, but that the possibility of a positive appropriation is left confidently to the history of faith as it will work out in the future. If there is—and none of us doubts this—a real history of faith, a history of dogma and not merely a history of theology, we cannot expect this history to take precisely the same form at exactly the same time in all the Churches, but can only assume that this lack of simultaneity is accepted by all the Churches.

I am quite sure that the Roman See in our time cannot merely rest secure in the possession of its traditional self-understanding, as it has done on the whole hitherto, until the other Churches come to recognize what we believe to be the legitimate authority of the Bishop of Rome, but must itself—even though apparently at great sacrifice—do something actively to bring about an agreement on this question. Certainly no Roman theologian has hitherto supposed that every individual power and every concrete style adopted by the popes over many centuries in fulfilling their task and exercising their authority pertained unambiguously and necessarily to the dogmatic nature of the Petrine ministry. But the Holy See itself has not hitherto made much effort to bring out clearly in practice the distinction between what must be absolutely firmly held as a matter of faith by the Catholic conscience and those matters of doctrine and practice relating to the Roman primacy which are time-conditioned and can be given up if a particular situation requires this. The paper I have handed to you attempts to make this distinction with reference to the teaching primacy. On this theme here are one or two further remarks.

Gentlemen, dear brothers in Christ! I think I can appreciate the difficulties you feel in regard to the teaching authority of the Pope as accorded to him at the First Vatican Council and left unchanged at the Second. At the moment we may leave aside the two Marian dogmas proclaimed by Pius IX and Pius XII, since it has been made clear to us on other occasions that the objective content of these two Catholic dogmas are not necessarily to be rejected by non-Catholic Christians as absolutely incompatible with their faith. As we already said, there can be mutual agreement on the fact that purely exegetical investigations or historical investigations carried out by methods of purely secular history do not lead to a joint conclusion. For—I would like to say—the real difficulty of non-Catholic Christians is in regard to *future* possibilities, to conceivable future *ex cathedra* decisions by the Pope. In this connection, even though they are prepared in principle to recognize a Petrine ministry, such Christians think that they are not in a position to make out a kind of blank cheque for the Pope in regard to the future. It does not seem to them to be clear and unequivocal that divine providence, which keeps the Church in the truth of Christ, is necessarily bound to be victorious in its effects when the Pope defines something and not at another point and in a different way. To the non-Catholic Christian it seems that the Catholic concentration of the victorious grace of truth promised to the Church precisely on a particular and juridically determinable act of the Pope is a human materialization of the grace of truth. This legalization seems incredible to these Christians also because, according to the evidence of history, on the one hand the ordinary magisterium of the Pope in authentic doctrinal decisions at least in the past and up to very recent times was often involved in error and on the other hand Rome was accustomed to put forward and insist on such decisions as if there could be no doubt about their ultimate correctness and as if any further discussion of them was unbecoming for a Catholic theologian.

I wanted to say this once and for all without prejudice and explicitly, since even the Second Vatican Council did not speak clearly enough about such authentic but reformable Roman doctrinal decisions and since Roman procedure after the Council left something to be desired by way of straightforward clarity and modesty. Purely theoretical arguments on our side have little prospect of success in practice in face of these inhibitions on the non-Catholic side. But—and this is my firm intention—here in Rome we can attempt to show more clearly and in a more mandatory fashion than hitherto that the concrete mode of procedure before and for an eventual papal *ex cathedra* decision in future will certainly be of such a kind that a non-Catholic Christian will not need to fear in practice and concretely that his blank cheque will be filled in with a papal teaching that is bound to be opposed to his conscience in regard to matters of faith. I am determined to codify a precise and transparent procedure defining exactly how the course of decision-making must run in Roman doctrinal decisions, if and as far as these decisions can still be expected in the future. Obviously I am prepared to accept suggestions as concrete as possible in regard to the content of such norms of procedure. At the moment however I want only to explain to you again briefly why such a procedure, although it does not yet exist, is compatible with the self-understanding of the Roman teaching primacy in the form binding on Catholics.

First of all it is a clear and conciliar teaching that a Pope even in *ex cathedra* decisions does not receive any new revelation from heaven. Consequently, when preparing for a doctrinal decision, the Pope must make use of all the human means at his disposal in this particular situation. But the moral norms implicit in this principle can be more clearly articulated and codified today in view of the present situation and the opportunities it offers. I would like to suggest what these norms could and should contain in at least one respect. When we learn from the First and Second Vatican Council that the Pope is infallible in an *ex cathedra* decision and that such decisions are irreformable of themselves and not in virtue of the consent of the Church, this merely means that these definitions do not acquire their definitive validity only by the *subsequent juridical* verification of their correctness by a higher legal authority in the Church, distinct from the Pope. But nothing of this implies anything more precise about the way in which such a papal decision itself comes to be.

The First Vatican Council also shows that papal infallibility is not independent of the irreversibly victorious promise of God to the Church as a whole. In an *ex cathedra* decision the Pope acts as head of the Church and of the whole episcopate as an authority that is restricted by the Church as a whole and its infallible faith. Consequently, in preparing *ex cathedra* decisions, the Pope must necessarily have recourse to the sense of faith of the whole Church, not in the form of a public opinion poll, but by looking to what is truly the Church's sense of faith. If such a recourse were not necessary, the Pope would need to appeal to a new revelation. But the Pope does not possess or receive any such revelation. He is the authentic spokesman of the Church's sense of faith and for this he has the assistance of the Spirit, an assistance which must not be understood as psychological inspiration, but which must mean the success, actually coming in the last resort from God, of his appeal to the infallible sense of faith of the Church as a whole. This reference to the whole Church's sense of faith of course takes different forms at the different stages of the Church's history in the light of the opportunities available at any particular time. Today certainly an explicit recourse to the episcopate as a whole is absolutely morally necessary from the nature of the case. Today also this recourse is possible in the most varied ways. But it is not now merely a laudable practice, maintained also by my predecessors Pius IX and Pius XII (perhaps in ways that were not satisfactory in every respect), but an absolute requirement. Such an explicit appeal is technically quite feasible today, even apart from a general council. But in that case it is also a moral obligation. For how could the Pope today say honestly that he had done what was humanly possible and morally required to acquire a human certainty that his teaching was a part of the Church's assured sense of faith if he had wanted to dispense with this inquiry which is quite feasible at the present time?

It is obvious that such a consultation today would have to take place in certain forms now possible of explicitness, transparency, facilitating dialogue, discussion with theologians, investigation of the believers' sense of faith, and so on—in a word, in straightforward sincerity and making use of the publicity now taken for granted—even though I must admit that even up to recent times these procedures have not been considered clearly enough or practised in Rome, as is evident from a glance at very recent dogmatic declarations by the Congregation for the Doctrine of the Faith. If such procedures were clearly articulated, expressly laid down as binding and applied in practice, if moreover in addition to the consultation of the episcopate as a whole there were included a consultation of the more important church leaders whose Churches had entered into a union with Rome respecting their independence, the papal decision emerging from all this would be both a decision of faith of the Church as a whole and also a papal *ex cathedra* decision in the sense of Vatican I. With such procedures even non-Catholic Christians would no longer need to fear an arbitrary manipulation of the papal teaching authority opposed to the Spirit of Jesus and of the Church.

My dear brothers, I must ask your patience for a second consideration. The Roman Catholic faith in the existence of a papal teaching authority, which in principle is always involved in the permanent nature of the Church, even though it has not always been clearly explained, does not imply that the actual exercise of this authority is the same at all times—even in the past this was not so—nor does it imply that it is independent of any historical and consequently varying preconditions. Because of the way in which the history of dogma of the first two millennia of the Church has usually been interpreted, we Catholics are accustomed to regard it as an increasingly progressive unfolding and articulation of the ultimate substance of faith in an increasing number of fresh individual explicit articles and consequently involuntarily to see the papal teaching primacy as actively involved in the emergence of these new and differentiating articles. Hitherto we have involuntarily assumed that the exercise of the Pope's teaching primacy, when he spoke *ex cathedra,* took the form of an explanation and laying down of articles which, although in the last resort implicit in the tradition of faith, nevertheless appeared to be somehow materially new and as previously scarcely explicitly palpable, as—for example—the two Marian dogmas of 1854 and 1950. But it seems to me that it is completely unproven and not at all probable that the papal teaching authority will continue to be exercised in this way in the future. The future history of doctrine of Christianity and the Church does not seem to be tending towards a further material differentiation of the substance of the Christian faith, but towards a new expression of the ultimate basic substance of Christianity, corresponding to the mental climate and sociopolitical situation of today and tomorrow. Consequently, it would be necessary to consider also how the papal teaching authority should be exercised in its diverse grades up to the highest if it is to endure into the future.

I do not need here to put forward an exact justification of this prognosis of the future history of dogma or, consequently, of the concrete way in which the papal teaching authority will be exercised. I would otherwise have to provide a more precise analysis of the mental climate of the world, of the present-day irreversible pluralism in a world that is nevertheless one, and thus clarify the assumptions drawn from secular history which affect the experience of faith of the world-Church today. Of course, this is not possible here. I appeal simply to your experience, brothers. In fulfilling your task, you all find that the message of the gospel offers a real hope for the future only when its innermost redeeming and liberating basic truth emerges from a direct, vital contact with men and the world as they are today and will be tomorrow. From that standpoint, I think, the future concrete exercise of the papal teaching primacy cannot be and cannot seek to be anything but a defence and up-to-date new statement of the basic substance of Christianity, that is, of the faith which is as obvious to you as it is to us Catholics.

I do not want to pursue further this perspective of the future with reference to the material content of the papal teaching primacy. But if this perspective is on the whole correct and if the formal way of exercising this teaching authority is clearly and juridically assured also by the Roman See, then, I think, for non-Catholic Christians there is no longer any reason in *this* respect to refuse to enter into a union even with the Roman Church, leaving entirely open the question as to whether these other great, particular Churches, living in unity and peace with the Roman Church, also have to proclaim explicitly the doctrine of the papacy precisely in the form presented to us in Vatican I. If a concrete and practical agreement on the papal teaching primacy, on the lines I have just indicated, could be attained among the Christian Churches, it would not alone remove all difficulties felt by non-Catholic Christians in regard to the Pope.

What has been said does not of course answer the whole question of the concrete exercise of the power of *leadership* in regard to the whole Church as this is claimed by the papacy. But we have made progress on this question in the past twenty years, since even according to explicit declarations the Apostolic See is convinced that the future unity of the Church will not mean reducing all the Churches to a uniformity modelled on the present-day Roman Church of the West, but that the particular Churches in uniting with Peter may and should retain to the greatest possible extent their own laws, their fidelity to their own tradition and history, that even in regard to the mutual recognition of ministries such an agreement has been or can be attained in a form which the Apostolic See thought it could not accept even a short time ago. This however is no part of the theme at the present moment.

My dear brothers, I am leaving you alone for today. For it may be a good thing, without regard for me, for you to discuss with each other the questions which the memorandum I presented to you and the remarks I have just made attempted to answer.'

SPONTANEOUS REACTIONS

The Pope took leave of the others with very little ceremony. The whole team had got to work so well, each one knowing everyone else, that no one thought it odd that all the former court ceremonial had disappeared. The other churchmen present stayed on, formed themselves into different groups and went on talking to each other. From our observation point in the background we could see that the conversation continued frankly and honestly, without bothering about subtle theological assurances. Admittedly I was able to catch only fragments of the conversation and I cannot now recall exactly who said the things that I managed to hear. To repeat: it was clear from their tone that none of them wanted to proclaim eternal truths or issue solemn decrees, but only to give their first impressions and explain their spontaneous reactions. Then one of them (I think it was an African) said: 'O God, I really can't understand why the whole thing should be such a terrible problem. Although we want to retain the autonomy of our Churches, we do really want *one* Church. And, while we co-operate in a "parliamentary" spirit, it is obvious to us that a concrete, living person must be the bearer and representative of this unity and must naturally have something to say about it. It would really seem ridiculous to me if we were to set out afresh to discover a representative of this kind, when we know from the history of the Church that one is already available.' He laughed and said: 'Perhaps that does not sound like very profound theology; there is really nothing in it about the nature of the Petrine ministry in the light of faith; we can leave it to others to think that one out. But why should not this simple consideration impose on me an obligation of coming to a realistic, concrete arrangement with the Roman See, so long as the latter requires from me no more than I can honestly give?'

Another person, who gave the impression of being a subtle theologian of the European style, began what almost amounted to a theological lecture. It could be seen that he was still under the influence of anti-Roman feelings from former times. This is more or less what he said:'We have been listening to an account of a shrewd strategic retreat on the part of modern Roman theology, but that is not to say that this retreat is not acceptable or cannot be taken seriously. But what did we hear exactly? The Roman See hitherto and even at the Second Vatican Council insisted that an *ex cathedra* decision is infallible "of itself " and not in virtue of the consent of the Church. Now the Pope has simply placed this consent of the whole Church—which he had rejected—*before* instead of after the *ex cathedra* decision. Verbally he has not given up anything that he formerly claimed and yet he has admitted that we are right. He has got himself out of the noose. And who are we to object to this?'

A third, evidently from the West, but looking a little more 'spiritual' than the second speaker, disagreed with this. 'I do not think', he said, 'that we can regard the Pope's declaration today in this way. After all, he justified his new attitude entirely with arguments drawn from his own tradition and always recognized as the starting point in Roman theology, even though no one had hitherto drawn from them the conclusions which the Pope put forward today and which he is prepared to put into practice.This sort of thing should not be suspected as a Roman trick. What in fact is happening is that progress is being made towards a unification by which it will become clear that it is possible to remain faithful to our own decision of faith without having to reject that of the others. As a result of this progress, after centuries-old obscurities, we can now see clearly that many more truths, the real meaning of which need not be abandoned, can enter into the one truth of Christ, more at any rate than we had hitherto thought, when we assumed that we had to interpret these many truths as contradicting each other. If the Pope really clearly, transparently and—for all men of good will—palpably refers the decision he has reached back to the faith of the Church as a whole, we ought not to pronounce a decided "No" to the teaching primacy of the Pope.'

In my dream the churchmen's conversation continued in this way for a long time after the Pope's departure. It roused hopes because the impression evidently prevailed that a more concrete offer had to be made in response to the Pope's suggestion.

My dream had come to an end. When I told a friend about it, he suggested drily that it was the sort of dream that could be expected of a teacher of theology. For only someone who was forever teaching could make people go on talking so long in a dream: it was not a real dream pointing to a glorious future, but the continuation into the night of theological reflections begun during the day. But I maintained that it was better to dream of something that could be realized and realized soon than to dream in a general way of a future of the Church that no one could foresee. My friend said: 'Let us hope that you have dreamed of something that will really come about in a few years; at present, unfortunately, it does not seem likely.' But we may dream and hope.

11

THE SPIRITUALITY OF THE CHURCH OF THE FUTURE

OUR THEME is 'spirituality', not an easy topic for discussion. The term itself is not by any means clear, but 'piety' or 'devotion' is even less apt to express the reality. Spirituality is a mysterious and tender thing, about which we can speak only with difficulty. As intense self-realization of the Christian reality in the individual person as individual, it is inevitably very different in every Christian, according the natural disposition, age, life-history, cultural and sociological milieu, the ultimate free and never wholly comprehensible uniqueness of the individual. For that very reason our theme is an exacting one and difficult to cope with. Moreover we are to consider the factors characterizing the spirituality of the Church of the *future* as such. But what do we know of the future of our history? What do we know of the future of the Church? Despite all modern futurology, how little can we predict the secular future? How far is the future of the Church also beyond the scope of the planning and calculation of its people and ministers? Because of their formal authority and the unchangeability of their proper message, the latter are of course always liable to think that they are the masters of the Church's history and can make unambiguous plans and issue clear directives; or, on the other hand, they might think that in the last resort nothing really important or surprising could happen, because in the ocean of history the Church is built on the rock of God's eternity.

What far-reaching changes however of the most surprising kind do in fact take place in the Church! How little did we older people and ministers of the Church, who grew up in the Pian epoch of the Church with its monolithism, how little did we expect a Church of the kind we have today? Those who brought Vatican II to a close wanted to break with the triumphalism of the Pian epoch and at the same time in a singularly ingenuous way and almost joyously proclaimed an *aggiornamento* of the Church in the world of today and tomorrow. How little did they reckon with what is going on in the Church today, something the Council did not cause but for which it acted almost as a catalyst? It is therefore almost impossible to speak of a future spirituality in the Church, since this spirituality is in fact also related to the unforeseeable destiny of the Church in its individual parts and in its totality. All this must be kept in mind from the beginning if we want to try to cope with this theme.

Nevertheless, we may venture to approach this theme directly if somewhat boldly. We are speaking—it must be made clear—of spirituality only in the Roman Catholic Church. From the outset, therefore, we are leaving aside the spirituality which obviously exists also in other Christian Churches as well as in the non-Christian religions, even though a good deal of what we have to say about this Catholic spirituality of the future may be true also of course of these other spiritualities and *vice versa*. We are leaving aside also the question—important enough for its own sake—about the changes Catholic spirituality may expect to undergo in the future as a result of the fact that the Christian Churches are coming closer together by their ecumenical efforts and that a more intensive interchange between the religious history of the Christian Churches and their future spiritual experiences is becoming possible. In dealing with our question we are also assuming without prejudice the faith as and in so far as it is proclaimed with ultimate binding force by the Church and its magisterium and as and in so far as we interpret appropriately this faith and the obligation it imposes, and grasp it as the firm basis of the spirituality of which we have to speak. In view of the impossibility of clearly predicting the future of the Church in the concrete and its future secular historical and sociological situation, we must not and may not be too worried as to whether we are talking of a spirituality existing or able to exist even now or of one that is coming into existence only tomorrow; whether and how far we are speaking of something that exists or will exist or only of something that ought to be today or tomorrow, whether we are proclaiming realities or unrealized ideals.

For a Catholic the *first* thing to be said about a future spirituality is quite obviously that, despite all change coming or to come, it is and will remain, albeit in a mysterious identity, the old spirituality of the

Church's history up to the present time. Consequently the spirituality of the future will be one related to the living God, who has revealed himself in the history of humanity, who has established himself in his most intimate reality—even as basic ground, as innermost dynamism and final end—at the very heart of the world and the humanity created by him.

Christian spirituality of the future also will be about the God of Abraham, Isaac and Jacob, the God and Father of Jesus Christ. This spirituality can never and may never degenerate into a mere humanism of a horizontal type. It will always be a spirituality of adoration of the incomprehensible God in spirit and in truth. This spirituality will always be related to Jesus Christ, the Crucified and Risen, as to the ultimate, victorious and irreversible self-promise of God, historically manifested to the world; it will be a discipleship of Jesus and will receive from him and from the concreteness of his life a norm, an internal structural principle, that can no longer disintegrate into a theoretical morality; it will always be an acceptance of the death of Jesus who, without any reassurance and yet absolutely openly, allowed himself in his death to fall into the abyss of God's incomprehensibility and incalculable decrees, in faith, hope and love, so that in this way and no other we attain to the infinite truth, freedom and salvation of God.

The spirituality of the future will also always be one living in the Church, receiving from it, giving itself to the Church, founded in it and sustaining it, even though it is as yet perhaps very uncertain what this implies exactly and concretely in the future. Such a spirituality of the future will also always be one that finds concrete expression and an ecclesial manifestation historically and sociologically in the sacraments of the Church, even though the concreteness of the relationship between the existentiality and the sacramentality of the self-realization of the Christian as such is in principle very variable even now and consequently can change considerably in the course of history. The Church's spirituality in the future—for the Church must always have a spirituality—will also have a sociological, political dimension facing on to the world, bearing a responsibility for this merely apparently secular world; and it may be said at once that this very dimension—which also pertains to spirituality as such—will in future presumably be more clearly possessed and filled up by the latter.

The spirituality of the future will be a spirituality of the Sermon on the Mount and of the evangelical counsels, continually involved in renewing its protest against the idols of wealth, pleasure and power. The spirituality of the future will be a spirituality of hope, awaiting an absolute future, enabling man to be grimly realistic and continually to break down the illusion that he could himself, by his own power and shrewdness, produce in this world and in its continuing history the eternal kingdom of truth and freedom. The spirituality of the future will always preserve the memory of the past history of piety, will regard as stupid, inhuman and unchristian the view that man's piety is continually making a fresh start—unhistorically—at zero and consists in nothing but wild revolutions.

This future spirituality therefore will learn over and over again positively and negatively from the Church's past. On the one hand therefore it will always, as in the past, be open for new pentecostal beginnings emerging from the base, not organized and regulated from the outset by authority from above, but bursting out charismatically where the Spirit breathes as he wills, even though such new charismatic departures prove in the discernment of spirits to be truly produced by the Spirit, since, apparently hoping desperately and almost self-destructively, they also establish themselves humbly in the institutional Church without having first negotiated legalistically principles to ensure that they do not perish in this Church of institutions. The spirituality of the future will always be lovingly and familiarly immersed in the documents of the history of the piety of past times, since this is its own history. It will never leave aside as of no interest to itself the history of the saints, of the liturgy, of mysticism; in the future it will perhaps also develop quite new forms of evangelical fellowship and yet have love and sympathy for the spirit and concrete form of older religious orders which are still alive. The spirituality of the future will preserve the history of the Church's piety and will continually discover afresh that what is apparently old and past can offer the true future to our present time. That was the *first* thing to be said about the spirituality of the future. This first statement of course does not exclude but includes the possibility that many individual forms and shapes of the piety of the past in their concreteness are no more than what has been and the Church must have the sober courage forthrightly to abandon them.

A *second* thing can certainly be predicted of the spirituality of the future: compared to the spirituality of former times, it will certainly have to concentrate very clearly on what is most essential to Christian piety. Since what is essential and decisive in the Christian faith was more or less taken for granted and undisputed in our cultural group of the western Church, during the past 1500 years, in public opinion and in society even in its secular fields, that faith was of course living and found expression in spirituality, but, really became interesting and attractive only when it ceased to be merely obvious and took concrete shape in the most varied individual types of piety, often in competition with one another. Devout people were deeply interested in the most diverse forms of devotion, particular religious practices, greatly varying styles of the religious life, each clearly distinguished from the others. For example (and all this is merely by way of example), succeeding one another and alongside one another, there were devotion to the Precious Blood, devotion to the Child Jesus and to Mary's Seven Dolours, a thoroughly organized intercession for the Holy Souls, an intensively cultivated practice of indulgences, etc.; clearly distinguished from one another were the very diverse spiritualities of the individual religious orders, the varying trends and tendencies in mysticism and their theological interpretation, a widespread practice of pilgrimage, the veneration of certain sanctuaries and miraculous pictures, and interest—sometimes scarcely intelligible today—in particular dogmas and theological opinions reflected in the piety of the time, etc.

All this will certainly not simply disappear from the consciousness and the life of the Church as such. For it can be observed that Rome even today is trying to keep alive some of these concrete individual forms of devotion. It would also be deplorable if everything were to disappear in a grey homogeneous spirituality and no one can say whether new and surprising concrete forms and practices of spirituality may not take shape in the future. But, in a bleak age of world-wide secularism and atheism, it may be presumed that far fewer individual flowers of Christian spirituality will be able to bloom. In this situation, even in the field of spirituality, concentration on the essential Christian beliefs is unavoidable and indispensable. There will certainly be Marian devotion and the veneration of saints in the future. And we can certainly only wish—and indeed in the light of the ultimate grounds of faith—that something of this kind will exist and even take on a new life. But we shall speak of Jesus and not of the Infant of Prague. We shall speak of Mary but have less to do with Lourdes and Fatima. In the future also there will be a eucharistic piety, including (we may hope) adoration of our Lord under the sacramental species. But this does not mean that the eucharistic cult with all its developments will retain in a living spirituality of the future the same position as in the past. I do not think that the piety of the future will have the same interest in new dogmas as was the case—for example, in the field of Mariology—up to our own time.

The spirituality of the future will be concentrated on the ultimate data of revelation: that God is, that we can speak to him, that his ineffable incomprehensibility is itself the very heart of our existence and consequently of our spirituality; that we can live and die with Jesus and properly with him alone in an ultimate freedom from all powers and authorities; that his incomprehensible cross is set up above our life and that this scandal reveals the true, liberating and beatifying significance of our life. These and similar things were not lacking of course even in the spirituality of former times, but they will make their impact more clearly, more forcefully and with a certain exclusiveness on the future spirituality of a bleaker age. Why should not this be so, if man and the Church actively realize that they are not masters of their history, but must so shape their spirituality that it is adapted to the historical situation imposed on us and not made by us and consequently should be credible even for non-Christians. Even this statement is of course burdened with all the reservations that are involved in the unforeseeability of the future.

There is a *third* point to be made. The spirituality of the future will not be supported or at any rate will be much less supported by a sociologically Christian homogeneity of its situation; it will have to live much more clearly than hitherto out of a solitary, immediate experience of God and his Spirit in the individual. Of course as such and in principle *fides qua,* which stamps all spirituality, has always been understood as an event involving personal responsibility, the decision and freedom of the individual. For this decision of faith in particular is less than anything else in a person's existence something for which he can shift responsibility to others, to other causes or to other causes preceding it. But formerly this act of faith on the part of the individual took place within a homogeneously Christian milieu, even though of the secular and bourgeois society; it was possible to believe what was believed by more or less everyone at least in the public sphere and in verbal communication, so that it almost seemed as if a person was relieved—particularly in the dimension of faith—from the supposedly untransferable burden of responsibility, of the decision of faith against unbelief, of hope against all hope, of unrewarded love; and in the area of spirituality it was a question only of the intensity by which we ourselves choose on a particular occasion what is taken for granted by everyone. Today it is different.

Christian faith today (and consequently spirituality) must be continually freshly realized: in the dimension of a secularized world, in the dimension of atheism, in the sphere of a technical rationality, declaring from the very outset that all statements which cannot be justified in the light of this rationality are meaningless or amount (in Wittgenstein's words) to 'mysticism' about which we can only be silent if we want to retain our integrity and sobriety.

In such a situation the lonely responsibility of the individual in his decision of faith is necessary and required in a way much more radical than it was in former times. That is why the modern spirituality of the Christian involves courage for solitary decision contrary to public opinion, the lonely courage analogous to that of the martyrs of the first century of Christianity, the courage for a spiritual decision of faith, drawing its strength from itself and not needing to be supported by public agreement, particularly since even the Church's public opinion does not so much sustain the individual in his decision of faith, but is itself sustained by the latter. Such a solitary courage however can exist only if it lives out of a wholly personal experience of God and his Spirit.

It has already been pointed out that the Christian of the future will be a mystic or he will not exist at all. If by mysticism we mean, not singular parapsychological phenomena, but a genuine experience of God emerging from the very heart of our existence, this statement is very true and its truth and importance will become still clearer in the spirituality of the future. For, according to Scripture and the Church's teaching, rightly understood, the ultimate conviction and decision of faith comes in the last resort, not from a pedagogic indoctrination from outside, supported by public opinion in secular society or in the Church, nor from a merely rational argumentation of fundamental theology, but from the experience of God, of his Spirit, of his freedom, bursting out of the very heart of human existence and able to be really experienced there, even though this experience cannot be wholly a matter for reflection or be verbally objectified. Possession of the Spirit is not something of which we are made factually aware merely by pedagogic indoctrination as a reality beyond our existential awareness (as great theological schools, especially of post-Tridentine theology asserted), but is experienced inwardly. This cannot be explained here in detail and at length. But the facts are there: the solitary Christian makes the experience of God and his liberating grace in silent prayer, in the final decision of conscience, unrewarded by anyone, in the unlimited hope which can no longer cling to any particular calculable assurance, in the radical disappointment of life and in the powerlessness of death—if these things are only voluntarily borne and accepted in hope, in the night of the senses and the spirit (without, as the mystics say, being able in this respect to claim a special privilege), etc. All this however assumes that he accepts the experiences merely indicated here and does not run away from them in what is in the last resort a culpable fear; under these circumstances he really has the experience, even though he cannot attempt to interpret it or give it a theological label. It is only in the light of this experience of God, which is the real basic phenomenon of spirituality, that theological indoctrination by Scripture and the Church's teaching acquires its ultimate credibility and existential enforceability.

As we said, this personal experience of God,[1] cannot be more precisely explained, described or—better—invoked. In so far, on the one hand, as it is the very heart of all spirituality, while we on the other hand are asking here about the peculiarities of the spirituality of the future, we shall examine some typical characteristics of this original human experience of God in both transcendence and grace which will belong (or belong even now) to this spirituality of the future.

We may now attempt to describe a *fourth* characteristic of the spirituality of the future which is part of a singular dialectical unity with the third, the solitary experience of God on the part of the individual. What we mean is the fraternal fellowship in which the same all-sustaining experience of the Spirit becomes possible: fraternal community as a real and essential element of the spirituality of tomorrow. By this is meant a phenomenon perhaps only slowly becoming clear, something of which we older people can speak only hesitantly and cautiously while still awaiting its future. I think that we older people did not formerly perceive what is meant by this phenomenon or at best perceived only traces of it, even though in looking back over the whole course of the history of spirituality it is possible frequently to discover something of the kind. By origin and education we older people were spiritually individualists, even though we gladly carried out the communal liturgy as our obvious, objective duty. Even though the phenomenon we mean, apparently being revived occasionally today, might also be discovered as existing in former times, on the whole the experience of the Spirit properly so called,

---

[1] Cf. K. Rahner/P. Imhof/H. N. Loose, *Ignatius von Loyola* (Freiburg 1978), pp. 10ff.; ET: *Ignatius of Loyola* (New York/Toronto/London 1979), pp. 11–13.

spirituality in its true sense, 'mysticism', was understood and lived as obviously a purely individual occurrence for one person and for himself alone occasionally in solitary meditation, in the individual experience of conversion, in the course of a retreat, in the monastic cell, etc.

Where was there a communal experience of the Spirit, clearly conceived, desired and experienced, in a general way—as it evidently was at the Church's first Pentecost—that was not presumably an accidental local gathering of a number of individualistic mystics, but an experience of the Spirit on the part of a community as such? Such a 'collective experience' cannot and of course is not meant to take away from the individual Christian his radical decision for faith coming from his solitary experience of God nor to spare him this, since human individuality and solidarity are not factors to be balanced against each other nor can they replace each other. But this is not to say that an experience of the Spirit in a small community is as such *a priori* inconceivable, even though we older clerics at least never or scarcely ever experienced anything of this kind and still less attempted to practice it. Why should it not happen? Why should not younger people and clergy now and even more in the future have easier access to such a communal experience of the Spirit? Why should not—as part of the spirituality of the future— phenomena like joint consultation among Christians, genuinely human communication in truly human and not merely external technical dimensions, events in group dynamics, etc., be embraced, exalted and sanctified by a communal experience of the Spirit of God and thus become a truly fraternal fellowship in the Holy Spirit? For this kind of thing in the last resort does not need to take place under extravagant accompanying circumstances apparently almost of a parapsychological character, such as are seen occasionally in American enthusiastic groups of the Pentecostal movements. There is no need to speak in tongues, no need to attempt to produce any phenomenon of healing by laying on of hands. In tomorrow's spirituality also sound psychology with all its critical conclusions must remain valid. But even if this factor is not naively ignored, even if not every kind of singular eruption from consciousness or sub-consciousness, not every transmission of insights and feelings from one person to another, is immediately interpreted as an inspiration of the Holy Spirit, this is far from saying that there cannot be anything like a communitarian experience of the Spirit at all.

Why could there not also be jointly a really spiritual discernment of spirits? Is the prayer to the Holy Spirit at the beginning of a consultation between Christians concretely and practically merely a pious opening ceremony, after which everything goes on as otherwise at a secular board meeting with the management making use of purely rational arguments? In the spirituality of the future can there not be a kind of guru, a spiritual father giving to another person an instruction filled with the Spirit, which cannot be completely broken down into psychology, theoretical, dogmatic and moral theology? In the spirituality of the future as such, I suspect anyway that the element of a fraternal, spiritual fellowship, of a communally lived spirituality, can play a greater part and be slowly but courageously acquired and developed. I have no recipes to offer as to how exactly all this might happen. But this certainly does not mean that there are no starting points and ways of access for such a spirituality in fellowship as such, even though a critical transposition of group-dynamics and similar occurrences into a truly spiritual happening is still to be sought, even though communal prayer as an external rite and communal Scripture reading as the study of exegesis by several people together and an instructive sermon in the traditional sense do not constitute that communal spiritual event which is here envisaged as an important element of future spirituality.

In conclusion, a *fifth* element of the spirituality of the future may be mentioned here: it will have a new ecclesial aspect. Regarded abstractly and in principle, this ecclesial character of Catholic spirituality is in itself something that must be taken for granted at all times, since we are talking about a spirituality rooted in a common faith and always to be sacramentally realized. But there is no need to deny or conceal the fact that this ecclesial aspect of a Catholic spirituality in the future will take a form somewhat different from that to which we were accustomed, especially in the last century and a half of the Pian epoch of the Church. At least once in this period the Church was the object of an almost fanatical love, regarded as our natural home, sustaining and sheltering us in our spirituality, where whatever we needed was available as a matter of course and had only to be willingly and joyfully appropriated. The Church supported us, it did not need to be supported by us.

Today all this is different. We do not see the Church so much as the *signum elevatum in nationes,* as it was acclaimed at the First Vatican Council. What we now see is the poor Church of sinners, the tent of the pilgrim people of God, pitched in the desert and shaken by all the storms of history, the Church laboriously seeking its way into the future, groping and suffering many internal afflictions, striving over and over again to make sure of its faith; we are aware of a Church of internal tensions and conflicts, we feel burdened in the Church both by the reactionary callousness of the institutional factor and by the reckless modernism that threatens to squander the sacred heritage of faith and to destroy the memory of its historical experience. The Church can be an oppressive burden for the individual's spirituality by doctrinalism, legalism and ritualism, to which true spirituality, if it really is authentic and genuine, can have no positive relationship. But none of this can dispense the spirituality of the individual from having an ecclesial character, least of all at a time when solidarity and sociability in the secular field are obviously bound in the future to increase and cannot decline. Why then could not the spirituality of the future take the form of a superior, duplicate naivety, marked by wisdom and patience, which has an ecclesial character because of the fact and in the very fact that it bears and endures as a matter of course the misery and inadequacy of the Church? Even Origen in his day knew that the Pneumatomachians could not be allowed to leave the Church, but, in patience, humility, bringing about the descent of God into the flesh of the world and the Church, and in love, would have to establish their possession of the Spirit in the concrete Church just as it is and as, in spite of all necessary and due reforms, it will remain.[2]

This kind of attachment to the Church must be part also of the spirituality of the future. Otherwise it is élitist arrogance and a form of unbelief, failing to grasp the fact that the holy Word of God has come into the flesh of the world and sanctifies this world by taking on himself the sin of the world and also of the Church. The ecclesial aspect of the spirituality of the future will be less triumphalist than formerly. But attachment to the Church will also in the future be an absolutely necessary criterion for genuine spirituality: patience with the Church's form of a servant in the future also is an indispensable way into God's freedom, since, by not following this way, we shall eventually get no further than our own arbitrary opinions and the uncertainties of our own life selfishly caught up in itself.

Allowing for all reservations about the unforeseeability of the concrete shape of future Catholic spirituality, have I succeeded in naming some few perhaps arbitrarily selected particular characteristics of this spirituality? I can't be certain, but may I hope so?

2 Cf. K. Rahner, *Erfahrung des Geistes,* 2nd ed. (Freiburg 1977).

12

UNITY OF THE CHURCH—
UNITY OF MANKIND

1. The Concept 'Unity'

BEFORE DEALING with the essential theme, I would like first of all to put forward some more or less general reflections, enabling us to make a preliminary examination of a number of concepts that will be useful later when we come to the theme itself. In the scholastic philosophy and theology of the Middle Ages there are quite detailed and penetrating reflections to be found on the four transcendental notions: *ens, unum, verum, bonum* (being, one, true, good). For this philosophy, 'one' or 'unity' is a transcendental notion, transcendentality—that is, super-categoriality, super-regionality—being understood in the light of both the knowing subject and its object. For Aquinas the transcendentality of the notion of *unum* also directly implies the profound, obvious and simultaneously unmanageable axiom: *Non enim plura secundum se uniuntur*—plurality as such is not a ground of unity. That is to say: what is absolutely disparate, that which has nothing common in any respect, in any way, is impossible and inconceivable. And, conversely, everything that is, that is possible and conceivable, rests on an ultimate solidarity which both embraces the difference of existents from one another and the difference between existentiality and knowability, between subject and object, and means in the last resort what we understand by God: the unity that exists in itself, preceding all plurality and sustaining all diversity. (It should also be noted that the metaphysical monotheism, briefly indicated above, respected by all the great metaphysical systems, is of course not the same thing as the religious and theological monotheism which Christianity together with the Old Testament and Islam professes. But for the moment there is no need to discuss this.) In the light of this ultimate primal unity, every individual existent —whose true and not merely apparent difference from other things is presupposed here as a primal datum—necessarily possesses both an internal unity of essential elements that are nevertheless distinguishable from one another and also a real and untransferable relationship to whatever else is real.

2. Unity as Existing and as Task

If, together with the above assumption, we also assume that everything other than the divine primal unity itself is not simply present as wholly static but is part of a world of becoming, then, within this world distinct from God, we must necessarily distinguish several concepts of unity. In the individual existent there is a unity already present which implies both the positivity of the sensible unitedness of the plural essential constitutive elements together with the unity of quiddity and actuality and also the negativity of being different and thus delimited and distinguished from other realities. Without such a unity already present in the existent with its positivity and negativity, any meaningful individual statement as also subjectivity and responsible freedom would in the last resort be inconceivable. An integrating and delimiting unity thus present from the beginning does not exclude the relatedness of each individual existent to reality as a whole, nor does it ever deny a world of becoming in which every existent is dependent on all the rest, in which under the dynamism of absolute being evolution proceeds with qualitative leaps.

If and in so far as each individual existent with its initial unity belongs to a world of *becoming* and unity is a transcendental determination of every existent as such—that is, must also belong to the goal of this becoming itself—then to every existent there belongs also a unity imposed on it *as a task,* a *unity still to be realized* as *telos* (goal) of its becoming. In its becoming every existent is oriented to a unity to be acquired, to unity as a goal of this becoming, even though the concrete content of the unity to be attained cannot be deduced from the formal and somewhat empty concept of unity, even though—where it is a question of the existing reality of the subject—the unity to be acquired is an act of freedom and of history, the content of which cannot simply be deduced from the unity already present, but must be realized and only in this way reaches an understanding of itself.

3. Unifying Unity

If and in so far as coming to be can never be understood as originating from empty nothingness, both the unity already present in the individual existent and also the unity imposed as a task must be understood as sustained by the unifying unity of the absolute being that we call 'God', so that the *already present unity* of the individual existent and the *unity to be acquired* of the existent coming to be presuppose an ultimate *unifying unity*. At the same time, as participating in the divine unity, *partial* unifying unities are wholly conceivable and even demonstrable in the world distinct from God.

Unity as the task of an individual existent can be related both to the greater internal unity of an existent and to a greater unity of such an existent with the rest of the world's reality. This duality of the unity to be acquired is not in principle self-contradictory; growing, reconciliatory unity of the internal, constitutive elements of an individual existent and reconciliatory incorporations of the realities outside the particular existent—in principle, at least—are mutually dependent. The unity to be achieved of an increasing interiorization and the increasingly far-ranging quest to include a wider environment are correlative. But this implies that the increasingly close approach to the unity to be achieved carries with it also a continual growth of the internal and external elements of that unity. In this way unity as task remains within the world of becoming and of history as such always as a goal approached merely asymptotically, never finally attained, since advancing unity is always producing new material that has still to be integrated into unity. The realization (even though asymptotically) of unity as a task, as distinct from the unity present from the beginning, is not an external, additional reality, but the completion of the initial unity itself; the history of the realization of unity as a task is the history of the unity present from the beginning, the latter being found again in the former.

4. Unity through Love

Corresponding to the transcendentality of the concept of unity, initial unity, unity as task and unifying unity, are analogical concepts which are realized or to be achieved in essentially different ways, depending on whether it is a question of the dimension of nature or that of the history of free subjects. In so far as the history of free subjects—although it cannot be reduced to the pure history of nature—carries with it the history of nature as an intrinsic element of itself and as environment, with the question of the initial unity and the realization of the unity to be achieved of the personal history of mankind, the counter-question of the history of nature cannot be left out of consideration.

Since however in the dimension of the free history of personal subjects unity as a task can never consist of a *homogenization* of the subjects that are its elements but only in a *reconciliation* of innumerable subjects, each different from the others and simultaneously (as subjects of unlimited transcendentality) possessing the whole in each individual and each in a unique way, the asymptotic realization of the unity to be achieved in the dimension of personal history can be produced only by what cannot be described except as *love,* not in the sense of mere sentimentality or as merely personal feeling but understood in a real and ontological sense. For love understood in this way is wholly the consummation of unity in accepting the absolute otherness of *everyone* else (in accepting *this* other as one's very own) and thus the reconciliation between universal unity and enduring plurality, which itself is accepted as good, as its own, by the loving subject.

5. Absolute Unifying Unity—God

Within a world coming to be and continually producing new plurality—plurality to be again unified and reconciled—in the dimension of free subjects and of history, unity as a task always remains a goal attainable only asymtotically. Consequently, without a fatal levelling out of the plurality and diversity of personal subjects, an absolute reconciliation and unity is conceivable only if the absolute unifying unity that we call God imparts himself to, reconciling and unifying, this plurality, and in this offer of himself by his own power is accepted also in the love of the plural realities of the world for one another and for this absolute unifying unity. This absolute reconciliation is not merely abstractly conceivable, but the innermost dynamism of reality and a goal to be victoriously attained: such is the faith of Christianity, for which unity is not merely always a still awaited Utopia but a real hope, since the unifying unity that we call God is not only the sustaining ground of the world's continually renewed will for unity, but has established itself in this world as the ultimate determination of the world itself.

In view of the transcendentality of the concept of unity it is obvious that everything said hitherto remains in an abstract vacuum. Indeed, in so far as all man's transcendentality and consequently his concepts are necessarily lost, yielding and being reduced to silence, in the absolute mystery of God and his incomprehensibility, this obscurity of all transcendental notions belongs necessarily also to the notion of unity, without the intellectual subject being permitted—overtaxed and frustrated—to dissociate himself from such concepts.

II. UNITY OF MANKIND

Under what we may hope is not an entirely false assumption, that the concepts just discussed and their correlations might be useful for our main reflections, let us turn, somewhat abruptly, to our more precise theme.

1. A Theological Theme

We shall look first of all at the unity of mankind, regarding this theme, not as merely philosophical or anthropological, historical or socio-political, but as theological. A theological statement about the unity of mankind is meant on the one hand to be understood as properly theological—that is, one made in the light of revelation—but on the other hand is concerned with a reality or task which at first sight we are accustomed to regard as secular, on which in theory and practice there are *others* besides preachers of the Christian faith and theologians who consider themselves competent. The theoretical question arising from this may not be very clear, but cannot be explicitly discussed at this point. If and in so far as Christian faith makes statements about what first appears to be a secular unity of mankind, while the authorization for such statements remains at present far from clear, we can be content at this point in our reflections with the fact that the statements are made as an *offer* to man's secular self-understanding so that it can be asked whether the latter is in agreement with them. If the offer is accepted, it could strengthen in a very radical way man's secular understanding of the unity of mankind, as long as it is assumed that the Christian message of this unity still retains considerable historical force at the present time and for the future.

The conviction of the unity of mankind is part of the Christian message. Perhaps today we take this belief very much for granted and perhaps also have the impression that we can manage without the agreement of the Christian faith in this respect, even though we are not at all sure what this unity of mankind implies and what not. If this is our impression, we ought at least to wonder, apart from anything else, whether its obviousness is not a secularized heritage from Christianity, a heritage which would be fatally threatened if once the sun of Christianity were really to sink entirely behind the horizon of history.

2. Biological Unity

Christianity however in any case declares its belief in the unity of mankind, regardless of whether this belief is to be understood as a proper and immediate object of Christian revelation or as an assumption with which —even though in itself secular—the essential content of Christian faith cannot dispense and which it consequently also affirms. This unity of mankind is first of all understood as a datum. Whether it reflects on this or not, whether it wants to be or not, mankind is one. The traditional statement about this original unity of mankind interpreted it in terms of what was known as monogenism—the doctrine that the human race as a whole descends from a numerically single human couple—which was strongly emphasized in Pius XII's encyclical *Humani generis,* then even prepared as a definition in a preconciliar scheme of Vatican II and later sank without trace at the Council itself.

If today we regard this biological monogenism as a model to represent the permanently valid unity of mankind and not as the actual content of the theological statement about this unity, we do not mean that the unity of mankind is no longer part of the content of faith. All that needs to be done is to interpret and substantiate it in a different way. We cannot explain it more closely here, but the fact is that this unity extends throughout all man's dimensions, finding appropriate expression at each point. Despite their biological descent from the animal kingdom, all human beings share a biological solidarity such that it clearly separates them from all—even higher—animals. They are all capable of reproducing their species with one another and only with one another. Their biological existence is not merely the basis of their authentic humanness and culture, but, conversely—unlike any other animals—it is in turn affected by these things. All human beings are able to enter reciprocally into a specifically human intercommunication and association in all man's dimensions. Actual barriers between geographically settled areas, between races and languages, in principle, can always and everywhere be surmounted. The differences of racially, geographically, historically conditioned mentalities do not constitute an absolute impediment to mutual understanding and cultural exchange in which individual nations each in its specific history can communicate and have always communicated with one another. By and large, whenever and wherever human beings recognize themselves as intellectually personal subjects with an ultimately unlimited transcendentality and thus as subjects of a free history, which always has also a religious dimension, and so too as moral beings with an absolute reciprocal moral claim; if then they cannot detect this particular kind of reciprocal relationship among other living beings in this world, they become aware of an exclusive unity on the part of mankind which is unknown among other—even biological—earthly realities.

3. One Salvation for All

Christianity radicalizes this existing and known unity of mankind with its teaching that all human beings , despite differences of race and history, diversity of cultures, are not only called into existence by one and the same God, but also have one and the same final destiny, which consists in attaining God's self-communication in itself. Christian faith is aware of a universal history of salvation, common to all mankind, existing from the very outset, always effective, universally present as the most radical element of the unity of mankind, not first slowly spreading out from a particular and regional history of salvation, but ultimately preceding the latter, which is no more than its particular and tangible manifestation. The universalism of the one salvific will of God in regard to all mankind, which establishes the final unity of mankind, is the sustaining ground of all particular history of salvation and religion.

Even at this point of our reflections more concrete questions could of course be raised, but we cannot enter into these now. Thus the question might be raised about a human, moral and Christian justification of racial intermarriage: a question which has not always been answered in the same way in Christendom, although it has not merely a secular human but also a religious and Christian aspect.

4. Sin

Christian teaching about the already existing unity of mankind involves further distinctions. It was pointed out earlier that this initial unity within the dimension of personal, free subjects and history is not simply static, but, as a task for mankind's historical freedom, has itself a history and thus can also be damaged and destroyed. The Christian doctrine of original sin, the full implications of which cannot of course be developed here, seems to me to involve the conviction that sin as selfishness, opposed to the unifying force of love, always and everywhere—not merely in the dimension of a personal interiority, but also in social life—affects the history of mankind and that this tragic situation will remain a permanent existential of mankind's history to the very end. But this means that the present unity of mankind is not merely not yet completed with the realization of mankind's unity as task, but is also damaged and disturbed, even though not simply destroyed, and will remain so—albeit in continually changing shapes and forms—to the end of history. Striving to realize the unity of mankind as task, an effort that always grows out of the sinful primal ground of history, will also continue in fact to produce new shapes and sociological objectivations of the disturbed state of mankind's unity.

From that standpoint the achievement of the unity of mankind as a task does indeed remain the goal always set before mankind in its history of freedom in the light of its initially present unity, but always retains at the same time the character of a Utopia never entirely to be realized within the course of history. Awareness of the permanent sinfulness of humanity—and thus of the always utopian and unattained pure realization of its unity—does not imply any authorization for adopting a static conservative mentality and renouncing both evolutionary and revolutionary attempts to realize a greater unity of mankind; but it forbids us to regard any concretely attained unity of mankind as pure, as absolute, as *alone* legitimate, and for that very reason really to lapse into a static conservatism.

5. Finite Unifying Unity

In the first part of these reflections we attempted, at least by way of suggestion, to gain some idea of a unifying unity. In an absolute sense of course God, and he alone, is the initially existing unifying unity, the dynamism of that unity which arises as a task, growing out of a unity already existing in mankind's history of freedom. But at least in the history of humanity there are also finite, particular and regional unifying unities. Over and over again in the history of mankind there emerge personal or sociological factors which, rightly or wrongly, claim not only to attain their own unity in themselves and in peace with their environment and with the people around them, but also to be for other sociological groups the bearers and protagonists of unity as a task. The claim to exercise such an unselfish function of a unifying unity towards others has often been made in the course of mankind's history. Those responsible include groups, nations, concrete supporters of a particular ideology, individuals.

Ancient Rome claimed such a function for its *Orbis;* Byzantium and, up to the nineteenth century, the Holy Roman Empire ascribed to themselves such a task for the peace and unity of human beings; in the ideologies of modern Spanish and Anglo-Saxon colonialism the idea of an active agent, a bearer of such unifying unity lived on. And today, when ideas of this kind of supremacy in the unselfish realization of a peaceful unity of mankind seem taboo, they continue to be secretly at work. In the sense of mission for freedom and order in the world continually revived by the U.S.A., in Moscow's claim to be the centre of orientation of the socialist world as a kind of 'third Rome', even today the ideas of the bearer of a unifying unity really live on.

If and in so far as Christianity, despite its proclamation of a universal salvation already present and effective everywhere, is also aware of a geographically and nationally particular bearer of this mission (ancient Israel, the primitive Church, Rome, etc.), it evidently regards the idea of such bearers of unifying unity as legitimate in principle and not merely as one that inevitably arises from time to time. The question might be raised at this point as to whether the older Europe did not give up too quickly and in too cowardly a fashion its claim to exercise such a function in regard to the rest of the world, whether it now sees its mission as consisting merely in defending itself as a consumer society, at the same time of course making excuses in a few well-chosen words for its abandonment of its former mission to the world.

Is unity—we must ask more precisely—even today still a task for mankind? And, at least as a goal to be approached asymptotically, in what is it supposed to consist? It cannot be disputed and need not be explained at length that, despite all disunity, all dissension and and all increasingly menacing conflicts, there is in practice in contemporary history a trend towards a greater unity. Histories of nations, formerly largely separated by a no man's land, are moving more closely to one another today; individual cultural groups, profoundly different among themselves, even today under the influence of a rapid development, are overlaid by a rational-technical world-civilization. Every political or cultural event anywhere in the world has a significance for all nations and regions of the world. Everywhere there are militant ideologies in the most diverse forms expecting and working to gain their victory everywhere in the world. There are the United Nations and industrial organizations that are supranational. There is cultural exchange to an extent formerly impossible, networks of news communication becoming increasingly closely interwoven, continually growing tourism, scientific organizations which are international by their very nature, and so on. There is no doubt that the unity of mankind is in fact growing.

6. Unifying Atheism?

It might be said that this fact, being concrete and inexorable, must also have its justification as a real task of mankind. We might therefore try also to justify at a deeper level as a truly human and moral task the pursuit of the unity of mankind: a unity which is being increasingly clearly realized. In accordance with what we said at an earlier stage, we could point to the fact that the differentiation of mankind, its cultures and mentalities—that is, the creation of a greater amount of material not yet united and still to be reconciled in unity—is increasing to the same extent and consequently that every success in achieving the unity of mankind in its turn creates new tasks. We could point to the fact that the unity of mankind as a task to be realized in history is always veiled by the unpredictability of history, where there is apparently no really palpable and absolutely effective individual authority planning in advance and effectively carrying out its plan for the whole course of history. We cannot deal at greater length here with this and many other matters connected with the unity of mankind as a task. All that we shall do is to point to some, mainly theological aspects of the problem as a preparation for the theological reflections on the unity of the Church that we still have to work out.

Wherever and in so far as it is realized, the formally and fundamentally legitimate unity of mankind as a task of its history is marked concretely by the stigma of sin. Since good and evil can never be clearly separated within the course of history, any unity that is achieved will always have something of the character of an enforced, oppressive unity; never and nowhere will it be purely the expression of conciliatory love and justice. It is from this standpoint, I think, that the permanent theological significance of the saga of the Tower of Babel becomes intelligible. The separation of peoples and languages, rendering impossible any attempt to unify the histories of individual nations, can be seen as a barrier set up by God's salvific providence against a collective revolt by a humanity united against God. Is it surprising then that, at the same time and to the same extent as mankind becomes united and as collective representatives of unifying unity again make their appearance in order to achieve this unity, a militant atheism comes to the fore, hoping and aspiring to become the one 'world-religion' of united humanity? The representatives of such an atheism and the incentives to it are very varied even today; its prospects may be very diversely estimated; a theological interpretation that discovers in it a positive function for salvation-history need not be excluded. But this world-wide and militant atheism as an obvious sociological phenomenon is nevertheless something radically new in the history of humanity, even though the believer is sure that the very person who claims to be an atheist cannot from the very outset be entirely deaf to the silent call of God. At any rate for the theologian of the history of humanity, at the point where the unity of mankind as a task is beginning to be realized, atheism is a phenomenon that he cannot lightly dismiss on the plea that there have always been atheists and now there are a few more of them. The unity of mankind and atheism as a sociological phenomenon have something to do with each other and theology must think hard about this, if on the one hand it explains the growing unity of mankind as a positive task for mankind but is aware at the same time that it is thus inevitably forcing faith into a situation which has never hitherto existed.

7. Unifying Christian Europe?

The unity of mankind, increasingly prevailing today, started out in fact from what was once Christian Europe. Rational and technical civilization, with its sociological and political power-potential, is of European origin; the West was the bearer of the unifying unity which inaugurated the realization of the task of uniting mankind. None of this is altered by the fact that this bearer did not merely or primarily regard itself as the representative of a Christian mission, but as the bearer of a technical and rational civilization which it thrust peacefully or forcefully on mankind as a whole, particularly since this secular civilization had itself essentially Christian origins, even though its distortions and consequences cannot simply be blamed solely on Christianity as such with its desacralization of the world. But the question then is: What is the theological meaning—that is, what is the meaning for salvation-history—of this fact, which certainly no one will simply and forthrightly dispute? Despite the necessity of making careful distinctions in answering this question, it can certainly be said that Christianity—whose active missionary bearer was in fact Europe as set between the great spatial blocks of Asia, Africa and America—through this united civilization for the whole world proceeding from it, but becoming itself depraved, actually even though largely unintentionally created the concrete conditions to enable Christianity to become a world-religion.

None of this can be regarded as a matter of course, since even a group of nations without a Christian history could be conceived in principle and abstractly as active bearer of the unification of mankind. But on the other hand it is actually and concretely scarcely conceivable that Christianity should acquire a real presence (which is not necessarily the same thing as a majority) in the world as a whole by a purely verbal mission without the substructure of a historical, cultural and civilizatory intercommunication between Christian and non-Christian nations. The global mission of Christianity may not strive (as it often has done) for a homogenization of the nations, following the European pattern, and by and large did not in fact achieve anything of this kind. But this in no way alters the fact that Christian missionary work not only made its own contribution to the unification of mankind, but itself needed concretely and practically a greater historical and cultural unity of mankind of a secular character and that this greater unity itself in fact started out from the Christian nations, whatever very secular, selfish and power-political motives may have inspired them. This is something that can certainly be given a theological interpretation. If it is to be realized, the universal mission of Christianity must presuppose a unity of mankind such as we are coming to know today: this unity the Christian nations created, even though always as sinful, selfish nations and while building this sinfulness of theirs also into it, a unity however which on its own account has a positive importance for salvation.

III. UNITY OF THE CHURCH—AND UNITY OF MANKIND

l. Church as Basic Sacrament

Now is the time, in accordance with our basic theme, to say something about the unity of the Church. We assume first of all that what is meant by 'Church' is not simply and solely the interior conviction of many of its members that God has offered himself as absolute salvation and absolute future in Jesus Christ, crucified and risen, and proclaimed this offer as historically victorious in word and sacrament. In fact, the Church has regarded itself always and everywhere as a real community and an institutional society, seeing this institutionality not merely as something humanly unavoidable but as its indispensable essential element, even though this essential 'visibility' of the Church has been diversely interpreted and put into practice in the different Christian denominations. It is only as such an historical factor in the word as proclaimed, in the sacramental word and the sociological character implied in all this, that it can be what it has to be: the permanent historical presence of God's victorious self-promise in Jesus Christ, the sacrament of the world's salvation, as Vatican II described it.

In order to be this basic sacrament, the Church must have an historical presence in the world to the end of time and do its utmost to carry out this mission to establish its presence *everywhere* in the world, even though of course nothing is yet decided in advance about the numerical extent of this world-Church and about its socio-political power, all this being left to the course of history itself which is not predictable even by the Church. The more mankind acquires a concrete unity, the clearer is the Church's character as basic sacrament manifested to the whole world, even when the sociological significance and the number of its members are very different in the different parts of the world. The particular question however with which we are obviously faced here is that of the Church's unity in face of its division and disintegration into many Churches and Christian communities which are not in communion with each other.

2. Scandal of Separation—Existing Unity

It must be admitted that the actual present-day divisions of the Christian Churches vary greatly in their theological and sociological character and it is also true that there are differences of opinion in both theory and practice about the exact nature and extent of the unity binding on all Christians. Nevertheless, for the Christian, according to the will of God, in the light of Jesus Christ and of the nature of the Church, the state of affairs is one that simply should not be. The sociological separateness of the Churches *as* Churches is a scandal that amounts to a terrible accusation against Christians in general and their office-holders in particular. On this there exists a theoretical unanimity in Christendom as a whole, since only a few Christian groups properly so-called are opposed in principle to ecumenical efforts to achieve unity; that is, Christendom as a whole acknowledges that its present state is an offence against the necessary unity of the Church.

This terrible scandal, a continual contradiction of the Church's mission, must not however blind us to the fact that, despite this sinful state of affairs, an initial unity has been maintained and remains effective to a very fundamental extent through God in Jesus Christ in the separated Churches. At least the Churches belonging to the World Council of Churches profess their faith in the triune God, in Jesus Christ as Lord and Saviour, practise one and the same baptism for the forgiveness of sins, acknowledge the same holy Scriptures as norm of their faith and life. However much—over and above all this—the reciprocal recognition of their ministries in the individual Churches remains theoretically a matter of dispute, my opinion is that the really dogmatic question remains open, even on the Catholic side.

Unlike the situation formerly, the unity of the Churches actually existing today means that they are not only co-operating in many tasks and at least up to a point join in united services, but also try in principle to distribute the blame for the divisions fairly among all the Churches and—over and above this—recognize in the separated and separately institutionalized Christian communities as such a positive salvific significance for their present members. All these things are constitutive elements of the actually existing unity of the Churches and are of fundamental importance. If then we evaluate all this according to the criterion proclaimed by Vatican II of the 'hierarchy of truths' and (we may add) realities, remembering at the same time (especially on the Roman side) that the unity of the Church set before us and still to be realized is not (as Rome thought during the hundred and fifty years of the 'Pian epoch') a uniformity of the whole Church, suppressing the peculiar character of the historically emerging and regional particular churches, then we may say without hesitation that the already existing unity of the Church is not as far from the unity which it is still the Churches' task to realize as we are perhaps tempted to think as a result of our certainly justified and impatient indignation at the scandal of divided Christendom.

This does not mean however that the scandal of divided Christendom has been eliminated. The existing unity of Christendom is not a static factor which cowardice and hopelessness might lead us to accept as final, but a factor which seeks and is bound to develop towards its full realization: that is, towards a unity set before us as a task to be fulfilled. What more can be said briefly here?

Christians, theologians and ecclesiastical office-holders should not assume that the divisions of the Churches have the same character today as they had at their beginning. Even ecclesial realities are essentially dependent for their concrete expression on the secular aspect of the historical and sociological situation in which they exist. Neither in regard to the expression of Christian truths of faith nor in regard to their sociological problems can any of the Christian Churches act as if they were still living at the time of the Reformation or even of the First Vatican Council.

3. Unity in the Profession of Faith

As far as the unity to be achieved in the question of truth and agreement in faith is concerned, the situation at the present time is substantially different from that of the past as a result of the work of the theologians in explicitly controversial theology and ecumenicism. If for the time being we exclude the question of the papacy, regarding this as part of the question of true or complete institutionality, then we can really raise today the question whether there are differences in matters of faith between the separated Churches which strictly require those who belong to the individual Churches to reject in conscience any unification between these Churches. My impression is that this is not the case. Of course, as against this impression, it is very difficult to say on the one side—the Protestant—what can be regarded as dividing the Church, as *articulus stantis et cadentis ecclesiae,* as 'an article by which the Church stands and falls', and by whom this can be decided; this is a deep problem, particularly since it is difficult here to identify anybody who can speak with final authority on the question. On the other hand, it must be seen that the Roman Catholic Church on the whole has never or only rarely interpreted in its official teaching (and not merely privately by the work of its theologians) dogma which it regards as indispensable from the time of Trent to that of the Second Vatican Council in such a way as to make this more understandable for Protestants and easier to assimilate in a positive reappraisal of its theology. Here, it seems to me, is a challenge to the authorities in the Churches on both sides; they cannot continue merely to invite the theologians to go on with their ecumenical work, while they themselves do little or nothing. It seems to me that the *decisive* initiatives and actions also in the dimension of truth, in the light of the present state of things, are required from the authorities in the Churches.

It also seems to me however that a piece of work for the theologians themselves, and especially on the Roman Catholic side, has not yet been done. To put it briefly and, unfortunately, not too clearly, what I mean is this: how, within this Church, a binding unity of faith and a new way of functioning to be developed by its magisterium on the one hand and on the other a pluralism of theology and interpretations of the one and binding faith, which simply cannot be avoided and cannot be adequately synthesized in the present mental climate, are compatible in theory and particularly in practice. Here, especially on the Catholic side, there remain deep questions that have not yet been answered, particularly in connection with the practical functioning of the Roman magisterium in the concrete, which—in my humble opinion—continues even today to make quite considerable mistakes: these are questions whose solution is of the greatest importance for a possible recognition of such a magisterium by Protestant Christendom. On this too however Catholic theologians must continue to work, but it really is time also for the Roman magisterium to be concerned boldly to explain and, especially in practice, to present itself in such a way that Protestants can have no justifiable excuse for not professing together with the Catholic Church the true basic substance of the Christian faith.

4. Unity and Institution

As far as the achievement of the unity of Christendom is concerned with institutions, the authorities in all Churches might be expected and required to embark in Christian hope on bolder plans, since in this respect also more seems possible than is actually being done in the present state of tacit acquiescence and stagnation in ecumenism. Here rank and file Christians in all the Churches should and could boldly seek from their authorities an opportunity to make their voice felt. Certainly they should avoid irresponsible actions which might lead in practice to a kind of third denomination: something that would not remove, but only intensify the divisions of the Churches. But if even an institutional unity is not merely an innocuous Utopia of the future but a binding obligation which is becoming increasingly urgent in the present historical situation of the world, then the authorities in all Churches—we might say, with the courage of despair and with keen theological imagination—should take action, even if only gradually, to establish an institutional unity of the Churches. In Rome the papacy should not be content to repeat the very general statements of Vatican II to the effect that, within the one Church, there is ample scope for a mutiplicity of particular Churches differing by reason of locality or of historical origins. Rome ought courageously and unselfishly to prove by concrete deeds that it is determined to renounce an ecclesiological monoculture in the Roman Catholic Church of the type attempted and largely realized especially during the Pian epoch of the Church of the last hundred and fifty years: a situation in which, in practice as opposed to official theory, individual bishops acted as petty administrative officials of the Pope of Rome and, for the sake of a supposed, but by no means necessary unity, were given no scope for any really important decision-making.

In this respect, as I said, the question of a reciprocal recognition of ministries seems to be more open than is usually admitted on the Catholic side. Of course, analogous questions and demands might be raised also before the Protestant authorities. But this is something that Protestants themselves must do. It seems to me that all that needs saying on this point can be stated as follows: Let the Roman Curia show bold resolution and dare to hope to achieve something of which the end-result cannot be calculated in advance, thus displaying itself in its ministries of teaching and leadership in a way demanded by the whole historical situation today; let it eliminate many features of a centralist and bureaucratically administered state, seeking to decree from above more or less everything that is at all important; let the limits of the universal primacy as they arise from dogma or can be restricted by the papacy itself be more clearly defined. If these things were done, I would hope that on the one hand the real substance of the dogma of the First Vatican Council could be fully preserved and yet that Protestants could see clearly that their evangelical freedom remains assured even within a united Church with a Petrine ministry.

5. Unity of the Church and Unity of Mankind

We must break off at this point. Our reflections should really be directed to the question of the relationship between a unity of the world still to be achieved on the one hand, and on the other a unity of the Church as already existing and as still to be realized. But perhaps we have said too little about this relationship, about this 'and'. At least however we may have touched on the essential point. The achievement of a greater unity of mankind is an urgent task for people today, if mankind is to survive and exist in a human way, even though this unity itself represents a mysterious and complex task, the precise meaning and content of which become clear only slowly in the historical process itself, and which is repeatedly debased by the sin of human beings and yet remains also their religious and moral task. The achievement of this unity of mankind is consequently also a task for Christians: not a mere side-interest for them, but a task for which all Christians and especially the authorities in the Churches have to answer before God's judgement.

What then might seem to be a purely secular task for Christians and their Churches—working to achieve the unity of mankind—has for them also a Christian aspect. By this work they create conditions to enable Christianity to become concretely a true world-religion or increasingly so, for the Church to become increasingly a true world-Church, for the Church to become increasingly clearly *one* everywhere in the world and thus more clearly the basic sacrament of salvation for the whole world. And, conversely, if Christians resolutely work and pray in an ecumenical spirit for the unity of their Churches, they will also make a very considerable contribution to the unity of human beings. The one dual mandate of the Christian for the unity of mankind and for that of the Church is not nullified by the fact that both unities continually and always in new ways carry with them conflicts and constraints detrimental to their true meaning, as long as the Kingdom of God is not present and God with the unity belonging to him alone is not yet all in all.

13

THE INEXHAUSTIBLE TRANSCENDENCE OF GOD AND OUR CONCERN FOR THE FUTURE

'HOPE IN the crisis of survival' was the theme of the ninth conference of humanists at Salzburg. Could a theologian be permitted to say something on this subject? The theme of the conference, after all, was about the future of our world with its history, which, according to Christian principles, is entrusted to man himself, to his freedom and responsibility, so that he may himself subjugate this world. Has the theologian anything to say in this respect that is not *either* a repetition of general humanistic principles and claims, which do not require a theologian to state them, *or* the proclamation of the God distinct from the world as a whole and of eternal life, which seems to make little or no contribution to the surmounting of our earthly crisis? On the other hand, in the notification of this conference as a whole and in many of its particular themes so much was said about religion and Christianity that we can almost take it for granted that the participants regarded these things as being implied in the theme of the whole conference on 'hope in the crisis of survival'; we can assume that this crisis represents a challenge to the Christian religion, that it alters this religion and at the same time provokes the latter's potential for hope, if it is to be overcome. If then it can be assumed that the theologian can and should seek an opportunity to contribute to the discussion, it is still not clear what he is to speak about. He has an almost inexhaustible number of themes from which to choose, as was clear from the theological implications of many of the papers delivered at this conference.

While recognizing that so many of these themes provide suitable material for a theologian, I would like to attempt—almost in a kind of

173

burlesque sermon—to say only one thing. The Christian message of God, who offers himself as himself in grace as our eternal life, is offered and brought to us as a message beyond earthly hopes and fears, beyond optimism and pessimism, but only on the absolutely indispensable condition that from first to last we do not make this God the instrument of our concern for the future and the amalgam of our neurotic fear of life, but succeed by God's grace in leaving God's transcendence (if we may put it this way) unexhausted. This (perhaps with a brief glance at the consequences for our own concern for the future) is all that I want to say and what I am trying to make a little more intelligible.

In the light of the average sermon in our churches we Christians are inclined to assume that human life in the long run and in society and history as a whole is impossible without God. World-wide atheism, whether of militant communism or of bourgeois indifferentism, takes a different view. But we Christians stick to our thesis and perhaps even cherish a secret hope that the world-crisis, which is becoming increasingly obvious, may provide many people with a new appreciation of this thesis. Of course, this conviction of the necessity and irreplaceability of God in our individual and social life is correct in the very last resort, if there is a God at all and if moreover this God is not, will not and cannot be, simply (and this is not immediately obvious) one who can make himself superfluous to the reality he sets up. But, even if we assume all this, the necessity of God and his usefulness for our own existence— particularly according to Christian principles—are much more mysterious and more difficult than the proclamation of a popularized, minimal Christianity would have us believe.

If all the questions coming into our mind find their ultimate answer only in the knowledge of God, while this God remains for all eternity the incomprehensible mystery, even when we come to see him face to face in the light of glory, what prospect is there of obtaining this ultimate answer? If God is supposed to be the ultimate target of all our deeds and ways, at which all our plans and calculations are aimed, while he is himself the mystery of an absolute freedom that cannot be fitted into a co-ordinate system in such a way that an understanding of the system would render this freedom also intelligible, how are clarity and palpable meaning to enter into these plans and calculations of ours? It is evidently not so easy to look to the true God of Christianity—who simply is not himself world-reason and this world's glory—in order to cope with our own existence and our concern for our future.

This God might equally appear to us to be the fundamental impossibility of 'solving' our own vital questions, whether individual or collective. All the more so since in the Christian message he has not offered himself as guarantor that all will always go well throughout our history, but as the finisher of this history—not only of the individual, but (as it seems, at least) of mankind as a whole—while the end of this universal history is represented in this revelation in its perspectives of the future in terms of catastrophe. The assumption is reinforced quite drastically by the fact that Christians are forbidden to hold the *theoretical* opinion that the future of mankind at the end of and beyond its history is on the whole and for everyone certainly a blessed consummation and that hell is *a priori* theoretically inconceivable. Seen in this way, does the word 'God', its acknowledgment of him, relieve us of any concern for the future, does it really brighten up our existence? Can we really invoke him by pronouncing this word, when confronted with the terrible existential fear which arises today in minds and hearts? If the God of Christianity is the incomprehensible God of unfathomable judgements, in our present distress, is it not better to leave him completely out of our calculations and instead to console ourselves with the thought that it will not be so bad without him and that we shall get along somehow?

In this darkness it is necessary to consider the true relationship between us and God, as acknowledged by authentic Christianity.

In order to see this relationship more clearly, we may begin with a preliminary general reflection on a particular kind of relationship which can exist between two realities, especially personal realities. It is easy to think that relationships or connections between two realities, being mutual, are of the same character or the same value on either side. But this is not always the case. The assumption of a particular relationship to another reality, if it is to succeed, may depend precisely on the fact that it does not intrinsically need to find a response of exactly the same kind from the other side. Without mentioning other examples of the most varied kinds, in order to understand what is meant here, we need only reflect on inter-personal love. If this is not to be selfishness in twos, love on the part of one must really be meant for the other, really for that person as such and in himself, and not for his importance to the one who loves him, not for the happiness he gives to the lover, not for the security he assures, but actually for himself, as he is meaningful, good and lovely for himself in his uniqueness, impregnability and unexploitability. That is not to say that it could not be expected, would not be hoped, that this other person, who is loved, would impart himself to someone who would respond to the love he received, would grant understanding, security and everything else that blooms in mutual love. But if in love in the last resort and tacitly what is sought is one's own happiness and the loved one is not loved for his own sake, if that loved one's gratitude is not accepted by the other partner as a wholly gratuitous miracle but was the very thing sought tacitly and without admitting it by one's outgoing love, then this love has already lost its true nature and been turned into selfishness, no matter how gratifying it now seems to be. True love is self-abandoning, never returning to itself.

The irreversibility of this movement of love is in no way changed by the fact that a person can be and must be the essence of such love and thus discovers his own true nature only by loving, is truly aware of himself only when he forgets himself in loving, gets at his real nature only when he succeeds in the miracle of getting away from it without any prospect of returning. This paradox is man's true nature. He takes in by letting go, he acquires stability by not seeking to avoid a fall; his happiness is attained only by seeking and finding something else; selflessness is the only way the self can come to be; man's most sinister temptation lies in the fact that he tries tacitly to turn unselfish love into an instrument solely of his own being. There is a genuine existential fear in the question which we ask ourselves and to which no amount of reflection can provide an answer: whether in the last resort we entrust ourselves in real love without any safeguards to the other person or make that person the means of our own happiness, which is the sole really definitive fixed point of our own existence.

We gave only one example of what was meant here, but it was not arbitrarily chosen and a more general description is not really very important: I know of no generally and immediately intelligible expression of it. Let us call it something like this: principle of the irreversibility of a relationship, of the non-congruence of reciprocal relationships, or (if the relationships as understood here involve something in the nature of a transcendence toward another) principle of the inexhaustibility of transcendence.

What has all this to do with the question that occupies us here? Normal, authentic Christianity proclaims that man's final salvation for all eternity can be gained only in the one love for God and men, love of God and love of neighbour being mutually dependent in a unique fashion on each occasion. What is meant in this teaching of normal and authentic

Christianity is real love of God and neighbour for their own sake, which, if it is to be truly love and productive of salvation, must be directed to God and neighbour in an irreversible and inexhaustible transcendence, not returning to itself and not being debased as an instrument for one's own self-realization.

How vast are the implications of this hackneyed catechism statement! Here are the benefactors of mankind, together with the futurologists and all the scientists, and the theologians intermingle discreetly and somewhat intimidated; all are asking, among other things, if God must still remain as an item in the world's accounts if these are to balance, whether we need God or not if we are to hope for a bearable future and avoid an apocalyptic disaster. Then, over this whole conference, where the completely understandable and legitimate egoisms of all people of the present time are accumulated, there appears the message of Christianity:

All your cares, all your fears, all your exertions, your futurological optimism and pessimism, your heights and your depths, your triumphs and your defeats, are ultimately pointless and doomed to destruction, unless in this whole history there occurs that one love in which we forget ourselves for God, love him for his own sake, adore him; unless we succeed in living in an irreversible and inexhaustible transcendence to God, with no prospect of a return. Christianity stubbornly proclaims that happiness, quality of life, a better or a sound future for the world, for mankind, are not the ultimate, obvious standard values governing our actions; and, if they are made such, will lead us into eternal ruin. Christianity knows that to will one's own reality, to be intent on self-development and to seek happiness, are legitimate enterprises and that this determination, even if it has not yet been transformed into a radical love of God for his own sake, is not for that reason alone sinful and hostile to God. But Christianity stubbornly insists that only love of God for his own sake will save us in the end. Christianity is aware of the apparently excessive and even absurd demands it makes on man and in the course of its history there have been enough attempts— deliberate or not deliberate—to reinterpret the inexorability of that love for God which tears man away from himself and thrusts him into God's incomprehensibility as into an unfathomable, dark abyss: new interpretations which turn all this into a sublime form of self-assertion in which a holy egoism can also be put—fortunately—at the service of God and thus be able to assert itself forever. Christianity knows and expressly states that this love for God, in which man must lose himself, is possible only by God's love approaching man and being itself offered from its innermost centre as the power of *that* love in which man has the courage to get away from himself, to abandon himself, as the only obvious thing to do: to allow himself to fall, to regard mystery as the true light illuminating everything, to know that death is the gate to life and that the love which seeks, not itself, but the God who is loved as such, means true life and eternity.

All this of course appears to demand too much of man. It is true that we can make sense of it in abstract, metaphysical terms by saying that man by his very nature is *a priori* that being which is related to the other, needing to get away from himself in order to discover himself, to forget himself in order to become truly aware of himself. But what kind of assurance does this metaphysical consolation provide in face of the all-too-obvious solid egoism, hardening hearts and apparently taken for granted in a struggle for existence in which victory is only for the strong and all ethics of selflessness and love apparently serve merely to conceal this selfishness at the roots of existence or to permit compromises between these egoisms, so that they become more bearable and offer more individuals a chance of survival? In face of the radical demand of Christianity for real love—without which there is no salvation—on the one hand and the monotonous routine of our earthly lives on the other, what is the use of this metaphysical consolation? Christianity cannot and will not relieve us of our deadly terror at this demand involving life or death; it offers no facile optimism, no magic by which from the very outset, as if it could not be otherwise, good people and criminals, murderers and their victims, are brought together into heaven.

In the course of its history however Christianity has rightly come to understand better than it did at the beginning that this incomprehensible love—the only love that is salvific—making apparently excessive demands on man can grow up mysteriously and as it were invisibly in many different shapes and on apparently completely unfertile soil. This love can be fidelity to one's own conscience, can be an ultimate, solitary unrewarded responsibility for others, can perhaps mean that composure by which a person, calmly and unconditionally hoping to the very end, submits in death to the inscrutable decree of providence and finds there shelter and protection. The mystery of salvific love, which draws us away into the sheltering mystery of God and liberates us from ourselves in order to make us free, can take on unexpected shapes and thus lead us to hope that there is more love at work in the world than our own experience might suggest, particularly since this experience can be clouded and distorted by our own selfishness isolating us from any encounter with real love. The fact remains that this love alone produces salvation and redeems man, the love that seems radically to overtax us. That is why, in the last resort, Christianity alone knows the answer to the terrible question of how man can escape from his prison of selfishness into redeeming freedom: the answer that God is greater than our hearts, that his promise of the victorious advent of his kingdom means that his love in its incomprehensible externalization can also accomplish the miracle of *our* love for him.

What then is the significance of this message of Christianity for the question of 'Hope in the crisis of survival'? First of all, the Christian message cuts right across the tasks and concerns of the kind of humanism seeking expression at this conference. It might be said—and of course quite rightly—that this conference is sustained and filled with that humanity which Christianity itself proclaims under the heading of true love of neighbour. Humanism and the love of neighbour it requires is understandably merely the rational harmonization of many egoisms, while love of neighbour only too readily makes use of the arguments of egoism, seeking to demonstrate (and this is very illuminating) that it is itself egoism properly understood and that love of neighbour properly understood will quite certainly never do any harm to one's own interests; a rational compromise between merely apparently mutually contradictory interests (it is claimed) is completely feasible. Yet, if we leave all this aside, it remains true that the Christian message offers and requires a real and unselfish love for God which is quite beyond comparison with the humanitarian device of the balance of interests. No, while recognizing a mutual dependence between love of God and love of neighbour, the ultimate message of Christianity cuts right across an intramundane humanism, since it involves a love for God in himself and for himself in which man simply does not pursue his own interests and the mutual balance of these interests, but in the last resort forgets his own assertion of himself above God, his glory and his honour; only in this way is God himself loved in himself and the 'advantage' of this love is for us merely the objective presupposition and practical consequence, but can never be what is sought in this love, can never be its motive.

The message of Christianity imposes on us at the very heart of our existence something utterly different from a humanism—however wise and however considerate of man's dignity—that tries to strike a balance between any conceivable primitive or sublime interests of men. This absolutely incomparable, disparate demand of Christianity on man is not for some sort of optional commitment; it is for something that a person must put at the very heart of his whole existence, knowing that, if God's kingdom is first sought, all the rest—as Jesus said—will be added anyway; and, if it does not seem to be added, this does not mean that he has attached too much importance to the love of God. Must not the Churches today make sure that their concrete proclamation in its emphasis and intonation does not blur what they have to preach as the first and last precept: 'Listen, Israel, the Lord our God is the one Lord, and you must love the Lord your God with all your heart, with all your soul, with all your mind and with all your strength' (Mark 12:29)? There can be no objection to world-responsibility, to intervention for justice in the world, for the Third World, for responsibility for the environment; no objection to protests against all violations of human rights and human dignity, no objection to involvement for the poor and oppressed. Declarations like *Gaudium et spes* are a good thing and even an obligation. There may be revolutions in which even the harsh exercise of power can be given a Christian justification. Theology may work out increasingly clearly and relentlessly the closeness of the link between love of God and love of men, may show ever more radically that the first commandment is implied in the second. But if Christianity is not to be stifled in the finite, God and the world must not be made to coincide simply in a dead sameness. And consequently there is a love of God that is not simply identical with love of men. We cannot behave as if only the death of God could bring man really to life. That is why we have the message of the absolute love of God from our whole heart and for God's sake alone, a love that is not simply summed up in the precept: 'Save the world!' This is the love that must be proclaimed in the first place by Christianity and its Churches.

Christianity would cease to exist if it no longer had the courage to speak of the blessed uselessness of love for God: absolutely useless, since it would not be itself if man were to seek in it his own advantage, his self-assertion, his own fulfilment. This divine uselessness of love for God, its inexhaustibility, the impossibility of turning back from the radicality of our transcendence to God, made possible by God in his Spirit: these things Christianity and its Churches must proclaim, aiming directly at the proud and despairing dialogue carried on by people about their certainly desperate worries and fears of the future. Where today are the prophets who cry aloud: 'Seek first the kingdom of God'? Prophets who do not confuse this kingdom of God himself with a more sublime plane of happiness and well-being in this world, prophets who do not make this proclamation merely because—one way or the other—they find this world quite bearable, but who raise their voice in the midst of apocalyptic fears?

However much the ultimate possibility and indisputable task of the Christian—and indeed of every human being—lies right across or even beyond his own concern for the future and his own fears for the future, within man's unity *that* task and *these* concerns have something to do with each other. This is what we have to speak about now. At the same time it is of decisive importance for the Christian interpretation of existence that man's inexhaustible transcendence to the incomprehensible mystery of God, his love of God for God's sake and not for the sake of man himself, should not again be tacitly reinterpreted as a useful, perhaps unrenounceable and necessary help for man himself in the problems of life. It is absolutely true that man needs God. But this need simply is not a justification of God. Indeed, if God were understood merely as a means and a guarantor of man's concern for himself, God himself would become unintelligible, for this very reason would cease to be the authentication and guarantor of man's humanity, could rightly be fatally struck by Feuerbach's opinion that he is only the projection of human needs and consequently would not exist at all. If then we ask what is the meaning for man of his inexhaustible transcendence to God in loving God for his own sake, it is a meaning that exists only when it is not sought for its own sake, when it does not put God at man's disposal, when God is loved not for the sake of this meaning but for his own sake, when the miracle of genuine love is realized, when its movement towards God does not spring back on man and does not again find its endpoint in man himself. Only on this assumption can all that is said about the meaning for man of his transcendence towards God be true and salutary. This at any rate is the way in which we can and must talk about this meaning. For—since God is a God of the living and not of the dead and despite the irreversibility of its orientation to God—love of God is not a love in which finite man is burned up and consumed, but a love that brings him to life, upholding and saving the person who loves unselfishly —precisely and only such a one.

This love of God for his own sake—which of course always includes belief in God's self-revealing self-communication and hope in the fulfilment of this self-communication of God, the inexhaustible transcendence of man to God without return—means freedom and what Scripture generally calls 'consolation'. Freedom: 'I am certain of this', says Paul

(Rom. 8:38–39), 'neither death nor life, no angel, no prince, nothing that exists, nothing still to come, not any power, or height or depth, nor any created thing, can ever come between us and the love of God made visible in Christ Jesus our Lord.' If this love is present, then the Apostle's statement is really self-evident. We are torn apart in this love by the immense variety and vitality of the powers that sustain, determine and threaten our life. None of these uncontrollable and incalculable powers and forces threatening our existence any longer takes first and last place in our lives; in this love we are ourselves grasped, sheltered in the infinite God of eternal fullness and security, infinity without a name, which is not the sum-total of the realities immediately encountering us. We are free, since there is nothing more that we set up as absolute, since there can be neither an absolute optimism nor an absolute pessimism in regard to the future.

The question is not whether in this love, which liberates us from everything, even from a precarious self-possession, we have infinite freedom in God, but only whether we actually *manage* to love God in this way. But this very love for God exists only when love's concern for itself is surpassed and relativized by love for God himself, when this love loves God and is not concerned with itself. And, since at the very heart of our existence God has revealed to us in the Holy Spirit and in the word of revelation in Jesus Christ that he is always prepared to bring about this love for him through his own Spirit, we can resolutely believe and hope that we love God, even though our impoverished hearts are scarcely aware of it and the miracle of this love is forever incomprehensible, if it is credible only to someone who—when the awful question arises—tries to take refuge in God's love itself and has the courage in the last resort to leave the question unanswered. But at that point there is freedom and peace. Nevertheless, this freedom in peace could never become in the present life a state of solid firmness on which we could rely as fixed and existing for all time. The situation is more like that of a swimmer whose head keeps appearing above the surface of the water that is threatening to engulf him.

In this continually fresh realization of love for God for his own sake, however, in which in the last resort we forget ourselves and the vulnerability of this love, freedom over all powers and authorities comes again and again as a sheer gift, and in this way alone comes also the one, silent consolation of which the New Testament speaks. Man today is tempted to make disintegration, unhappiness and despair the very essence of his life-style. But this is impossible when disintegration and unhappiness are really dominant and not merely an incidental phenomenon in an otherwise easy-going, contented life. Someone who is continually struggling to entrust himself in love, unconditionally, to the incomprehensibility that we call God cannot take up a triumphalist attitude—claiming freedom, peace and consolation as his indisputable possession—towards another person who does nothing of this kind and does not pretend to do so; nevertheless, he has these things because he has found God by losing himself in him.

Has this inexhaustible transcendence of man to God any impact on concrete life in space and time, in society and in history as it is experienced? This is our final question and we shall attempt a brief comment on it. Once again this comment must be preceded by a reminder that a positive answer to the question cannot be expected to provide a justification of this inexhaustible transcendence of man to God. Any attempt to justify man's transcendence to God in terms of its positive consequences in the world and in history and to make it a part of the present course of events would simply destroy it. Truth is useful; but if someone wanted to make utility the criterion of truth, he would miss the very truth that is most useful. Love creates happiness; but only if it does not seek its own happiness. God is our ultimate meaning, but only when this meaning is sought for its own sake and not as a means for our fulfilment. Only under this condition can what is still to be said be rightly done and consequently rightly understood.

Before agreeing to the 'usefulness' of this inexhaustible transcendence of man to God, however, a further preliminary observation must be made. I do not know whether world-history will continue as it obviously ought to continue, if mankind as a whole expressly and absolutely radically throughout all its dimensions is to realize fully that love of God, that radical self-commitment to the infinite mystery, which as such is required of it in principle. Perhaps if something like this were to be realized, we should have what Christians call the consummated kingdom of God, bringing this history to its end into the glory of God. It is therefore conceivable that the apparent or obvious lack or even decline of a transcendence towards God in this world has a positive meaning for the continuation of an earthly history and of the further development of mankind and its potentialities, even though it would remain or does remain true (as already indicated) that in this apparently godless world love for God is actually realized in a thousand forms and it is still possible to hope for the transcendent salvation of mankind as a whole. It remains true of course that anyone who is called and enabled to realize an intensive love for God cannot refuse the call merely because elsewhere world-history is perhaps continuing meaningfully even without such an explicit and intensive love. If then there is to be a positive answer to the significance of an inexhaustible transcendence to God even for the world and its history here and now, this does not mean that the course of this history will certainly be good up to a point or bearable only as long as this love for God occurs precisely in *those* forms and shapes which we have in mind when we speak of love for God and which are required from us in our own special situation.

We do not say once and for all, with regard to particular instances and possibilities, that the actual realizations of this transcendent love for God as such are under no circumstances detrimental to the realization of intramundane possibilities. If Pascal had not only remained healthy, but had also renounced his mysticism and his Jansenist theology, he would certainly have achieved results in mathematics and other secular sciences which he might be said now to owe to mankind. Moreover, it should not be claimed—however much it appears to be becoming again necessary, particularly today, for this earthly history—that man's inexhaustible transcendence to God itself alone could render superfluous all those intramundane objectives which must be jointly and freshly discovered, the absence of which we lament in the present great historical turning point brought about by technological developments. All this can be realistically and honestly admitted and must be respected, since otherwise all attempts to maintain the necessity of a religious significance of human existence would be dishonest.

Nevertheless, it can and must be said that if someone lives out his inexhaustible transcendence towards God, without expecting a reward, he is in fact 'rewarded' even in this life, even though he is not spared the bitter tragedy of individual and collective history which must be endured equally by both just and sinners. It is only through love for God that the norms for appropriate action in the world acquire practically and effectively the dignity of a commandment expressing the divine will and only in this way does it really become clear that respect for such commandments must be justified before the judgement seat of the God of absolute holiness. The intramundane relevance and the consequent requirement of ethical action may certainly not be neglected or bypassed. Nor is it very easy to explain why and how such a requirement of finite and relative values can emerge with the majesty and inexorability of an expression of the divine will imposing an absolute obligation. But, since there are such finite and relative values which come upon man as a divine requirement, moral action in the present world on the part of someone who loves God acquires for him a dignity and inexorability which undoubtedly determine in a specifically new way his intramundane action in accordance with these values and a motivation and an obligation that can only be beneficial to that action.

In addition to what has just been indicated, man's transcendence towards God confers a further significance on his action in the world: it relativizes and deprives his immediate goals and tasks of their idolatrous character. If we look dispassionately and without prejudice into contemporary history, we find in theory and in practice a shocking absolutizing of particular realities and possibilities, although this cannot be explained here in detail. This terrible trend to set up individual finite realities and values as absolute, to deify, to idolize, in order to have some absolute reality in the vacuum of lost meanings—not an absolute to which we surrender, but which we seek to control in order to exercise power—results in fanaticism of ideologies, the awful intolerance of social systems, the raging blast of propaganda, the arrogant and terribly stupid habit in politics of painting everything in either black or white. When man has no God into whose incomprehensibility he is willing to fall, he comes under the domination of particular idols, setting up monomaniacally rational calculation, technology, pride in being able to do everything, the perfect functioning of a system, sex, power, etc., absolutely as the only starting point and making them the sole criterion of action and life on each occasion. If someone does not and will not manage to love God for his own sake, apparently with nothing to show for it, he must necessarily absolutize a particular reality in its individuality and make it the final criterion; he must construct a pantheon with a supreme god, since otherwise he would become disoriented and be lost in the multiplicity of realities and possibilities seeking to become God. But such an individual god, even declared to be supreme god, remains an individual and the conflict between these gods would continue restlessly until the final doom of all. We may not set up anything individual, even ourselves, as absolute; we should attach absolute importance to everything and yet not attach absolute importance to anything; we should not think we know everything and can dominate everything; we must be able to set ourselves free without any guarantee, tested in advance, of getting anywhere and yet hope to do so (we might almost say) with childish simplicity; we must venture out into pathless incomprehensibility without fear of losing the way; we must really get away from ourselves.

If we do this, keep on trying, keep on believing that what we demand—with such an incomprehensibly excessive demand—from ourselves will be granted us, then we love God: only then do we understand anything of what is meant by this word; then the idolatrous images on our life's way are broken, even the idols we made of legitimate future planning and of only-too-understandable fear of the future. We know then that in our own existence and in the destiny of mankind, whether by life or death, we fall into the hands of the God whom we must leave nameless and of whom it can nevertheless be said that for us he is eternal light, eternal life, ineffable glory, peace without end, since he has enabled us to forget ourselves and to be for him.

INDEX